CAMBRIDGE LIBRARY COLLECTION

Books of enduring scholarly value

British and Irish History, Nineteenth Century

This series comprises contemporary or near-contemporary accounts of the political, economic and social history of the British Isles during the nineteenth century. It includes material on international diplomacy and trade, labour relations and the women's movement, developments in education and social welfare, religious emancipation, the justice system, and special events including the Great Exhibition of 1851.

Homes of Taste

Jane Ellen Panton (1847–1923) was the second daughter of the artist William Powell Frith, and a journalist and author on domestic issues. First published in 1890, this was one of a series of advice guides written by Panton on life and work in the middle-class home. With each chapter focusing on a different area of the house, the book offers advice to young married couples on how to make their homes 'tasteful without undue expense' by devoting time and effort to renovation and furnishing, and by choosing decorative styles that would not date. The author encourages her readers to become 'house proud', and to this end suggests that men should learn basic carpentry and refurbishment skills, while women should become proficient in needlework, as opposed to 'dawdling' over 'mere society flutter'. Providing a revealing snapshot of life in late nineteenth-century England, this book will appeal to social historians.

T0364273

Cambridge University Press has long been a pioneer in the reissuing of out-of-print titles from its own backlist, producing digital reprints of books that are still sought after by scholars and students but could not be reprinted economically using traditional technology. The Cambridge Library Collection extends this activity to a wider range of books which are still of importance to researchers and professionals, either for the source material they contain, or as landmarks in the history of their academic discipline.

Drawing from the world-renowned collections in the Cambridge University Library and other partner libraries, and guided by the advice of experts in each subject area, Cambridge University Press is using state-of-the-art scanning machines in its own Printing House to capture the content of each book selected for inclusion. The files are processed to give a consistently clear, crisp image, and the books finished to the high quality standard for which the Press is recognised around the world. The latest print-on-demand technology ensures that the books will remain available indefinitely, and that orders for single or multiple copies can quickly be supplied.

The Cambridge Library Collection brings back to life books of enduring scholarly value (including out-of-copyright works originally issued by other publishers) across a wide range of disciplines in the humanities and social sciences and in science and technology.

Homes of Taste

Economical Hints

JANE ELLEN PANTON

CAMBRIDGE
UNIVERSITY PRESS

CAMBRIDGE UNIVERSITY PRESS

Cambridge, New York, Melbourne, Madrid, Cape Town,
Singapore, São Paolo, Delhi, Mexico City

Published in the United States of America by Cambridge University Press, New York

www.cambridge.org
Information on this title: www.cambridge.org/9781108052962

© in this compilation Cambridge University Press 2012

This edition first published 1890
This digitally printed version 2012

ISBN 978-1-108-05296-2 Paperback

This book reproduces the text of the original edition. The content and language reflect
the beliefs, practices and terminology of their time, and have not been updated.

Cambridge University Press wishes to make clear that the book, unless originally published
by Cambridge, is not being republished by, in association or collaboration with, or
with the endorsement or approval of, the original publisher or its successors in title.

"STAINED FLOORS"

Without skilled labour, unpleasant smell, or waste of time. Floors can be stained and varnished in one operation without the trouble and annoyance of sizing, by using

JACKSON'S COMBINATION VARNISH-STAINS,

which dry hard in about twenty minutes, with a surface equal to French Polish. They can also be used over old floors that have been already stained and beeswaxed. Made to represent the following woods—

WALNUT, DARK OAK, LIGHT OAK, BLACK OAK, MAHOGANY, ROSEWOOD, EBONY, SATINWOOD.

PRICES—

Pints, 2s. Quarts, 3s. 6d. Half-gall. 6s. One gall. 10s.
Tins and carriage free.
Sample bottles 9d. and 1s. 3d., post free.

These Stains have been supplied to many of the best houses in the kingdom, and we are in possession of many hundreds of testimonials ; but we think it will be sufficient for readers of this book to know that scarcely a week passes without a recommendation of our Stains by Mrs. Panton in the 'Home' columns of *The Lady's Pictorial.*

We would also call attention to our special **Wax Composition**, for dressing the Stained Floors. This fragrant and lasting composition is most useful, and adds considerably to the wearing property of the Varnish-Stain. In tins **1s.** and **2s.** Circulars with full particulars as to brushes, etc., on application to the Works—

199, BOROUGH HIGH STREET, LONDON, S.E.

Established 1853.

SANITARY NON-ARSENICAL WALL-PAPERS.

LAND'S
93, Cannon Street, London, E.C.

Art Wall-Papers
AND
Decorative Materials.

Raised-Flocks ∴ Lincrusta ∴ Anaglypta ∴ Leathers ∴ &c.

Our Stock is the most varied in London, and the utmost attention is paid to obtain the most choice Designs and Colourings in all qualities of Goods.

Should your Builder or Decorator not have our Pattern Books, apply direct to us.

J. & H. LAND,
93, CANNON STREET, E.C.

CENTRAL SHOW ROOM—

Facing S.E. Railway and District Railway (Cannon Street Stations),
ACCESSIBLE FROM ALL PARTS.

THE

AUTOTYPE FINE ART GALLERY

74, NEW OXFORD STREET, LONDON, W.C.

THE GREAT MASTERS. Reproduced in Autotype permanent photography from the grand works in the Louvre, Hermitage, Uffizi, Madrid, Sistine Chapel, &c.

THE NATIONAL GALLERY, LONDON. Three Hundred and Forty-nine Examples ; and, by permission of H.M. the Queen, selections from the Royal Galleries of Windsor and Buckingham Palace.

AUTOTYPE REPRODUCTIONS OF MODERN PAINTINGS from the Salon, the Luxembourg and the Royal Academy.

THE GREAT BRITISH PORTRAITISTS. Reynolds, Romney, Gainsborough, &c., from choice Proofs in the British Museum.

THE LIBER STUDIORUM. Facsimiled in Autotype from fine states lent by the Rev. Stopford Brooke, M.A.

THE ART OF FRANCESCO BARTOLOZZI. One Hundred Examples, with Notes and Memoir by Louis Fagan, Esq.

IDYLLS OF THE NORFOLK BROADS. By P. H. EMERSON, B.A., M.B. Twelve Plates by Auto-Gravure in handsome portfolio, with descriptive letterpress. Proofs, £1 11s. 6d. ; Prints, £1 1s. 6d

OLD PARIS. Ten of Meryon's celebrated Etchings reproduced from choice Proofs in Auto-Gravure, with Notes by the Rev. Stopford Brooke, M.A.

THE GOOD SHEPHERD. CHRIST AND PETER. Autotypes of two noble drawings by Frederick Shields, R.W.S.

AUTOTYPES from the Works of G. F. Watts, R.A., Holman Hunt, Rossetti, &c., &c.

THE INDUSTRIAL ARTS OF PEACE AND WAR. By Sir F. LEIGHTON, P.R.A., from the Cartoons for the Frescoes at South Kensington.

ANCIENT ATHENS. Twenty-five Large Autotypes from Negatives by W. J. STILLMAN, Esq., issued by authority of The Hellenic Society. Prospectuses on application. Pictures framed in artistic style.

"The distinguishing character of the Autotype reproductions is that they are cheap and absolutely faithful copies of the originals, which may themselves be of the very highest excellence; and they are therefore, especially adapted for all situations in which the moderation of their cost is an important element, and especially for all in which it is desirable, for educational reasons, to keep before the eyes, either of children or of adults, the most perfect representations of natural or ideal beauty."—*Times*, September 4th, 1879.

Free by Post.—A Pamphlet, 40 pages, and 4 Illustrations.

AUTOTYPE: A DECORATIVE AND EDUCATIONAL Art. Containing a description of Autotype, Suggestions for Decorating the Home with appropriate Pictures, short Lists of Autotypes of the most celebrated works, with Illustrations of Frames and Mouldings, Press Notices, &c.

THE AUTOTYPE COMPANY, LONDON.

HOMES OF TASTE

BEAUTIFUL HOUSES;

At their Studios, Chesham House, qualified Architects, Artists and Assistants produce designs for all kind of Domestic Buildings, Specialities, and Novelties for interior Decoration and Furniture.

Also a responsible representative, with a folio of selected sketches, can meet clients by appointment, take sizes, submit suggestions for any work; and afterwards forward, free of charge, complete drawings with detailed inclusive estimate. A new handbook of sketches post free.

(*LIBERTY & CO., Chesham House, Regent Street, London.*)

HOMES OF TASTE

ECONOMICAL HINTS

BY

J. E. PANTON

AUTHOR OF "FROM KITCHEN TO GARRET," "NOOKS AND CORNERS,"
ETC., ETC.

" *Festina lente* "

LONDON

SAMPSON LOW, MARSTON, SEARLE, & RIVINGTON, Ltd.

St. Dunstan's House

FETTER LANE, FLEET STREET, E.C.

1890

[*All rights reserved*]

SOME RECENT BOOKS FOR THE HOUSEHOLD.

By MRS. HAWEIS.

The Art of Housekeeping : A Bridal
Garland. By Mrs. HAWEIS, Author of " Beautiful Houses," "The Art of Beauty," &c. Post 8vo, cloth, 2s. 6d. An *Edition de Luxe* of 250 copies, printed on handmade paper, suitable for presentation, 7s. 6d. each, nett.

Beautiful Houses ; being a Descrip-
tion of Certain Well-known Artistic Houses. By Mrs. HAWEIS. With a Preface. Third and Cheap Popular Edition. Post 8vo, boards, 1s.

By MARY HARRISON.

The Skilful Cook : A Manual of
Modern Experience. By MARY HARRISON. New edition, crown 8vo, 5s.

LONDON:

SAMPSON LOW, MARSTON, SEARLE AND RIVINGTON, LTD., .
ST. DUNSTAN'S HOUSE, FETTER LANE, E.C.

CONTENTS.

GODFREY GILES & CO.,

Artistic Decorators & Upholsterers,

19 OLD CAVENDISH STREET, W.

Sole Makers, Inventors, and Patentees of the Patent

"ANGLE" & "CONVERTIBLE"

COSY CORNERS.

Suitable for any Room. At all Prices.

WRITE FOR PRICE LISTS AND FULL DESCRIPTION.

FITMENTS

AND

INTERIOR WOODWORK

for Entrance Halls, Bedrooms, Drawing Rooms, &c. Plans and Estimates submitted in any part of the United Kingdom.

GODFREY GILES & CO. design Pretty Rooms, and estimate same free of charge for the Decoration, Woodwork, Furnishing, and Upholstering, and also for the Carpets, Curtains, &c.

GODFREY GILES & CO.'S lovely

WALL PAPERS

And CRETONNES to match are admired by all.

SAMPLES ON APPLICATION TO

GODFREY GILES & CO.,

19 OLD CAVENDISH STREET, OXFORD STREET, LONDON, W.

*Corner of Room fitted up by GODFREY GILES & CO., showing one of
their Patent Cosy Corners, with Canopy Top.*

HAINES. & CO.,

MANUFACTURERS OF

Artistic Wall Papers,

AND IMPORTERS OF

Japanese, French, and American Paperhangings.

Every description of Material for Home Decoration kept in stock at prices defying competition, including

JAPANESE LEATHER PAPER From 1s. 6d. per Square Yard.

ANAGLYPTA, The New Embossed Material for Dados, Walls and Ceilings, from 4½d. per Yard.

LINCRUSTA WALTON For Walls and Ceilings.

SILK, SATIN, AND CRETONNE PAPERS.

IVORY WHITE ENAMEL From 20s. per Gallon. Dries Hard and with Surface like Porcelain.

CRETONNES To match many of our Wall Papers kept in stock. Patterns on Application.

Dado, Picture, and Ceiling Mouldings

From 1d. per Foot.

DAMP-PROOF PAINT FOR DAMP WALLS.

Varnishes for every description of Interior Decoration, from 2/3 per Quart.

Samples and Patterns may be obtained through any decorator, or Post Free of

HAINES & CO., 83 Queen Victoria St., London, E.C.

HOMES OF TASTE.

CHAPTER I.

GENERAL PRINCIPLES.

UNDOUBTEDLY the first hint to be given here is, that nothing must be done in a hurry. If we desire our houses to be tasteful without undue expense, and if we wish our homes to be really charming, and in some measure a reflex of ourselves, and not the exposition of a certain upholsterer; we must not grudge time and trouble to produce this desirable end. Neither must we be unduly swayed by that which is the fashion for the moment, as, unfortunately, if we do, we shall soon become wearied by what is stamped with a certain date, and long for

B

something less absolutely marked as the pro-
duction of the year before last—or, indeed,
of the year before that! If we proceed to
decorate and furnish our house at the express
speed which is one of the worst character-
istics of the age; if we allow the builder to
cover our walls with hideous papers, which he
is anxious to " decorate" the house with; not
because they are charming, but simply for the
reason that he purchased large quantities at a
very low cost from some paper-hanger, who
was delighted to clear out unsalable goods at
merely nominal prices; we may as well give
up the attempt to be pretty and have a tasteful house; for vulgar papers are only accentuated by pretty furniture, and made even
more prominent than they otherwise would
have been, had the builder been allowed to
complete his work by turning in some upholsterer, as unscrupulous and as inartistic as he
is himself.

It is often most distressing to me to be
consulted on the subject of one of these
" builders' houses," for they all bear a hideous
family likeness, and it is invariably impossible

to do much to make the place better. But still more distressing is it to be consulted about a clean new house, to write down, or cause to be written down, the most elaborate directions for each room, giving name of papers and addresses where all are to be procured; and then to find that the owner has been talked over by the builder, who naturally objects to the tenant finding his own paper; for is he not deprived of the enormous discount of 33 per cent. taken off to the trade? or the still larger one he makes for himself, by buying up these species of "remnants," all marked legibly at the back for the benefit of the tenant, who does not understand that that especial price was what would have been charged (less the percentage aforenamed) had the paper been as successful as it was undoubtedly a failure; and that it has been bought up at a mere song, on purpose to spoil the house of any one who is foolish enough to ask the builder about papers, or who, to save trouble, goes to one special shop or establishment; and allows himself to be talked over by the shopman, who in his turn has "premium goods" to dispose of, and takes advantage at once of those whose innocence betrays itself immediately; and who often buy what they know they will detest, because they are not prepared to state which they really wish to have; and are not strong-minded enough to refuse to be talked over by a glib and plausible shopman.

Now in these days paper is so cheap, and is generally so pretty, that I cannot too earnestly impress upon my readers to absolutely refuse the builder's aid in any scheme of decoration they may have thought out for themselves; and I as earnestly ask them to take time about the selection of their papers; and to have some reason for all they cause to be put up in their abodes; for with charming papers ready to one's hand at one shilling and two shillings a piece, the poorest amongst us can have a tasteful house if he wills; and to obtain this most desirable end, need remember only one or two things—that his rooms should be one definite colour, and that they should in some measure harmonize with each other. The great reason why so many houses are still commonplace and ugly being that the builder has decorated the walls with a muddled paper—neither brown, green, nor yellow, but a mixture of all three—and that he has reproduced this mixture in the striped paint which he calls "picked out," and which is as absurd as it is ugly and inartistic.

Let us, therefore, first of all consider a house as it should be—the empty ungarnished house which I much wish every one could find ready waiting to their hands— and then think of the ready decorated builder's house; with its marble halls, or its even more ridiculous tiled paper with a paper dado; and its nondescript papers on the walls of the sitting-rooms; its sprawling colourless bedroom papers, which fade in one season; where the pattern rubs off on one's garments, and where the paint is a perpetual eyesore; and see how we can in the one case cheaply and artistically render the little house charming; and in the other how we can mitigate the horrors with which we are so often called upon to cope; and which always cause my heart to sink when I am called upon to legislate for

houses where no positive colour is to be found,
and where all resembles the nondescript cheap
and muddled tapestries; which are rapidly
vanishing, I am thankful to say, and giving
place to plain materials, or to materials pos-
sessing definite colours and definite designs.

Now I should much like to suggest that all
young men who may be in a position to marry
on a small income should be taught over hours
to paint, paper, and do simple carpentering
work. I see no reason why any one should
refuse to learn these most useful trades; and
only think what an advantage this would give
the would-be Benedick! more especially if he
yearns for pretty surroundings, and dreads—
as who does not dread?—the incursion of the
British workman into a house; while of
course he would have double the money to
spend if he could do the work himself, or at
least such a portion of it: that, instead of his
home being a jumble of odds and ends, it would
under his skilful hands become a vision of
beauty, and an exponent in some measure of
himself and his wife's tastes and ideas.

It does not require very much education to

be able to tell how much paper it takes to cover walls of such an amount of space, and the hand that writes down columns of figures can as easily learn to wield the paint-brush; and as Aspinall has reduced the science of painting to a mere mechanical process, where nothing is required save the hand to apply the paint to a prepared surface, my next piece of positive advice is : that all young men should be able to decorate their own houses, and to become independent of anything save their own skill and taste. Given such an education, add to that the capacity for making simple pieces of furniture, and house-furnishing is reduced to the very lowest amount of expenditure; the while we are saved the enormous worry of watching a tribe of men wasting their time, and our money in an equally lavish manner; and of knowing that after all the house will not be in the least what we want ; for how often do we pass over some quite vital mistake in order to rid ourselves of those who, once admitted in a house, seem to make up their minds to remain there for the rest of their lives? Now all these troubles can be saved if young men

learn at technical schools, or in ordinary car-
penters' shops, the simple processes of papering, painting, and carpentering ; and if the
girl he is about to marry can also wield the
needle and use the sewing-machine, the simple
curtains can be run together by her, and
the clean frilled cretonne covers made for
the drawing-room, which she can replace at
will whenever she thinks she requires new
covers to her chairs.

Let any one consider the absurd prices
charged for things made up, say dresses, or
chair-covers, or what you will, for the mere
mechanically papered and painted house, of
even the roughest furniture, and then let
them as carefully consider what their own
fingers can save them ; and I venture to state,
that instead of young men "killing time," and
young girls dawdling over ridiculous so-called
"painting," fancy-work, and mediocre piano-
playing, and mere society flutter ; we shall have
a race of "house-proud" young people, who
will devote all their thoughts to making their
homes charming ; and marriage will not be
quite as impossible as it appears to be now-a-

days for a good many, would both men and
women resolve to decorate their nests together,
and so render themselves independent of the
British workman. Even if the girl never
married at all, she would always be able to
keep herself, or at all events improve her
income, for the demand for clever workwomen
never ceases. And when a girl has really
some marketable talent, she can never starve,
or become an unwelcome burden on the
shoulders of the more prosperous members of
the family, which is, alas! too often the case
now-a-days, when parents have large families
recklessly, and leave their girls nothing save
the memory of an extravagantly nurtured
youth, which makes it doubly hard for them to
turn out, often in middle life, to face a world
which has nothing but the cold shoulder to
present to the unfortunate creatures.

Certainly one of the most necessary hints
for an economical house of taste is this one of
the useful education of the boys and girls who
have to live in it, for I have often been
troubled by the sight of a would-have-been-
charming house made ugly and dirty and

shabby by the very hands which, properly trained, would have been the very ones to keep dirt at bay, and which could have made it as beautiful as it was the exact reverse. Let me impress this emphatically on my readers who may long for artistic things, and dare not embark in them because of the work they entail; if they can do things for themselves, nothing is impossible; and given taste and clever fingers, the house kept up on £500 a year—the very, very lowest sum any lady and gentleman should marry on, in my opinion—can be as artistic and as beautiful in its way as the one maintained on as many thousands.

I always admire and much commend the old German plan of every girl beginning to collect for a home of her own from the earliest days. Silver spoons and forks, odds and ends of china, pictures and books are all given to her with this laudable end in view; and as soon as she can sew, a quantity of linen is bought, and she learns to hem sheets, make pillow-cases and table-cloths, and prepare a regular trousseau of house-linen, which in its turn she embroiders with beautiful letters and

monograms—these of course of her own initials
— thus obtaining slowly and surely what
would be out of her own power to procure
en masse should she marry in her own rank of
life. In England, of course, the bridegroom
provides the house-linen; but I think he
would not object to find that his bride had
her "dower-chest" of fine linen made and
marked by herself, and that her fingers were
as useful as of course he considers them
beautiful. Even if the girl never marries, she
would have material to furnish her own house
when she has to turn out into the world—a
turning-out which must come sooner or later
for all unmarried women who survive their
parents in the natural way.

A house of taste—the house of the future—
begins to be formed in the nursery, and is
made up in a thousand ways. The child who
has hideous surroundings, vulgar pictures
nailed up against an ugly common paper,
blinds which are never drawn up straight—
things provided more on the grounds of their
use than their beauty—will never care for its
own home, and will never learn to have taste.

Allow it to tear the paper off the walls, kick the paint for sheer naughtiness, and spill paint, ink, or any other messes all about the house, and it will never care for its own house when it comes to have one; but carefully train it in nice ways, allow it good colours to look at, and good pictures on its walls, and teach it to respect its surroundings, and I venture to prophesy that it, when it grows up, will have an intelligent love for its home, and will take care always to have beautiful surroundings. It may appear absurd to dwell at such a length on the artistic making of a house. " Souls are not saved by dados," says one; " friezes do not take one an inch nearer heaven," says another; while a third musingly remarks, " So long as we are clean, nothing else really matters." But I boldly contradict all these cavillers. I am quite certain that when people care for their homes, they are much better in every way, mentally and morally, than those who only regard them as places to eat and sleep in; and that heaven is much nearer those who regard beauty as a necessity, and who refuse to be surrounded with ugly things;

while if a house is made beautiful, those who are to dwell in it will care for it intensely, and will cultivate home virtues that cannot exist, unless they are carefully watched and tended in a place where ugliness is banished entirely.

Let us dwell, therefore, emphatically on the absolute duty of any one who is about to form a home, to make that home as lovely as he or she possibly can. A home has an immense influence, an influence that may never be known of to the individuals themselves, but that is none the less real, none the less of absolute service to all those who may be brought within its radiance; and therefore all those who are about to form a new house hold should recollect that by allowing hideous surroundings, or passing bad workmanship, they are continuing evils which, had they been less weak-minded, would have ceased to exist as far as they are concerned; and would have soon become obsolete, because nobody wanted them. In these days, except for the speculative builder, we have immensely progressed; in very, very few houses do the old

and ugly marble papers of twenty years ago
find room; that they have given place to even
paper dados marks a step in advance. But
I wish to go much farther; I wish to insist
on the necessity of doing away with shams
altogether—with the sham tiles in the afore-
said dado, the sham paper rail or strip of
paper which simulates a rail, with the abominable graining as hideous as it is imitative,
and with many other shams all more or less
ugly, all more or less attempts at being what
undoubtedly they are not; and as men are
really producing beautiful papers at very small
sums, and we have Liberty, Aspinall, and
other geniuses as regards decoration to go to
for hints, there is absolutely no need why the
humblest home in England should not be
charming.

Of course opinions are divided on the subject of what is pretty and what is not. Some
people really admire things which to me are
absolutely painful; but as long as they have a
reason for surrounding themselves with those
particular colours, far be it from me to say
emphatically that they must not do so. A

house to be a home should express the opinions and the taste of those who live within its walls; but let the owners have these opinions, and let them have these particular schemes of decoration because they admire them, and not because the builder has them to sell; or because it is too much trouble to select others which are more harmonious. And let me farther impress on those whose time is short, and who have no space in which to look about from shop to shop for their requirements, that it is far better to consult some one not an up-holsterer or decorator; but some one who has no interest whatever save the desire to do his or her utmost for the employer, who has the different papers and draperies at his or her fingers' ends, and who can submit immediately to them schemes of decoration, all more or less artistic, but all immeasurably superior to the ordinary villa-builder. Thus will the home be far more artistic and complete than it could have been were it left entirely to the tender mercies of a tradesman who has always some-thing he is far more anxious to sell, than he is to procure what his client really requires,

and who has been made so persuasive by long
years of selling, that he talks his unfortunate
victim out of his preconceived ideas, and so
brings into being another of those terrible
houses, without any definite colour or design,
with which our suburbs are over-crowded.

Having in this preamble put before my
readers some of the numerous stumbling-blocks
in the paths of those about to furnish, I will
now indicate shortly how a house may be
decorated artistically at a small cost, and also
farther indicate how, when a builder has done
his very worst for a house, one can judiciously
mitigate the horrors thereof in a manner that
shall not draw attention too forcibly towards
the walls, by contrasting with them too vividly,
and yet shall not make future improvements
impossible by saddling ourselves with hangings, carpets, and furniture which match the
builder's decorations, and are therefore too
frightful ever to have a better background
provided for them.

CHAPTER II.

HALLS AND PASSAGES.

THE usual builder's house has the invariable
builder's hall—the narrow miserable passage,
and the stairs put in such an engaging manner, that the moment the front door is opened
one appears to fall up-stairs ; and this hall is
furthermore generally charmingly decorated
with grained paint and the usual marble or
tiled paper. Now if the future inhabitants of
this chaste abode cannot afford to re-paper
and paint ; and tackling the hall even in quite
a small house is no light matter ; I strongly
advise that, at all events, the entrance portion
of the hall should have a high dado put round
of Liberty's wonderful arras-cloth : this should
be in the darkest shade of brown, brown and
yellow producing a very beautiful effect ; and

it should be nailed just above the skirting-board, in such a manner that the edge of the arras touches the wood, by light upholsterer's tacks, and should be fastened along the top by a light wooden rail, sold by Haines and Co., 83 Queen Victoria Street, E.C., for something under 1*d*. a foot; this rail should be secured to the wall by screws,—screws can always be removed, nails cannot,—and the rail should be painted Aspinall's nut-brown. The great expanse of graining on the hall-door, and indeed on any door which opens on the hall, can be hidden by a *portière*; this should be in golden-yellow serge, at 1*s*. 11½*d*. a yard, wide width. This should be simply hemmed, and hung straight down over the doors, should the doors open into the room; but should they open out into the passage, the curtains must be hung on Maple's door rods—these cost about 4*s*. 6*d*. each, and allow of the curtains opening and closing with the door in such a way that the curtain itself is never touched. If possible, just in the entrance, the wall above the arras should be papered with a clear yellow and white paper, such as Pither's "berry," at

2*s.* a piece, and even Maple's 4*d.* a piece yellow and white paper is preferable to the marble paper above the arras. This paper must only be used on the ceilings, unless placed above a real dado; it is "pulp," not paper, and in consequence bears no wear at all, and would soon rub into holes and become shabby were it placed low enough down for dresses, etc. to be constantly pressed against it. It is an admirable ceiling-paper, and could be used in the hall with the brown arras, taking care that whatever cornice there was was simply coloured cream, not picked out or coloured in divers hues, in the manner so dear to the heart of the ordinary decorator.

If the arras only is used,—and this covers a large space, being fifty-four inches wide, $9\frac{3}{4}d.$ a yard only,—the decorator's art should be turned on to the space above the arras, which should be covered as much as possible with the inexpensive open Japanese fans and screens, and here and there a bracket surrounded by and made more important by a trophy of fans, and supporting one of the wonderful Imari vases one buys for a few pence. Of course good

autotypes and engravings and photographs
are much to be preferred to these makeshifts,
and I most strongly advocate giving good
framed autotypes as wedding gifts instead of
the ornaments, and cheap jewellery, and endless salt-cellars and biscuit-boxes which are
all too often showered recklessly on the bride
of to-day. Autotypes of Turner, Gainsborough,
or any of the beautiful pictures one can procure at the Autotype Company's place in New
Oxford Street, forming in my opinion ideal
gifts, for they can never go out of fashion in the
manner that other things do, which have not
stood the test of years as these pictures have;
and to the ordinary bride in the ordinary
suburban villa silver salt-cellars are nothing
save a useless trouble. She has no butler to
keep them as they ought to be kept, and she
fears burglars, and dare not use them; while
judiciously chosen autotypes would have been
a joy for ever, and adorned her somewhat
commonplace little abode without any farther
trouble on her part.

If the arras is run round the hall it could
be easily put on, and the rail painted by the

husband; it is quite an easy piece of work,
and indeed I number among my acquaint-
ance a lady who has done this herself. It will
give him something to occupy him in an evening, and it will at once improve the hall,
making what was a most ordinary passage
into an artistic entrance. Very little graining
will show once the doors are covered; and if
the hall-floor is covered with self-coloured linoleum, with two or three Kurd rugs on it, and
the stairs with an artistic carpet without much
pattern or *any* border, the *tout ensemble* will be
very pretty, and disclose immediately to the
eyes of the caller that here is the abode of
people who care for their home, and wish it to
be pretty, and who thus denote that they are
worth cultivating, for no doubt they will turn
out to be desirable friends.

Of course if the hall be still undecorated,
there will be at once no obstacle in the way
of having a very pretty place. The arras is
the only manner at present invented of im-
proving the "marble halls" at small cost and
easily, but there are endless ideas for papering and painting in such a manner, that the

first exclamation made by strangers is, "Oh, how pretty!" But here let me begin by saying there are one or two axioms that may be laid down, and that must not be forgotten : the first is once more, keep all the paint an even surface of colour, allow no pickings out any- where ; and another is, that if there are no tiles put down one must have linoleum ; nothing takes its place, and where hard wear is to be expected, as it is in any passage, nothing is better than a plain dark-brown linoleum. At first, like all plain materials, it seems as if it were going to wear disgracefully—it shows every footmark, and sometimes looks as if it were going to crack ; but all it requires is judicious rubbing with boiled linseed-oil and vinegar mixed ; soap and water should never be used, though of course the dirt should be removed with clean soft water. And I farther recommend putting down some Kurd rugs, one or more, according to the size of the hall ; these commence in price at 8s. 9d., wear an immense time, and can be shaken daily, thus getting rid every morn- ing of the previous day's dirt and mess in a manner that is only possible where rugs are used.

I have myself tried every other material in a hall—felt, which is equivalent to casting one's money straight into the fire; carpet, which is never clean; and matting, which promptly wears out. Cocoa-nut matting never looks well, for even the crimson sort fades soon, albeit the wear is everlasting; so I have now reluctantly been forced to admit that the despised linoleum is the only material that answers every purpose; it is always clean, wears very well indeed if properly treated, and makes a capital background for the rugs, which, after all, make the hall as artistic in appearance as carpet itself would do. And I furthermore suggest, that the living room doors in all small houses, where the front door is not more than a couple of feet from the doors of the living rooms, should be curtained. This sounds a rash and reckless suggestion where money is an object, but the fact is, that one saves the cost of the material very swiftly, not only in comfort and immunity from catching cold, but also in the expenditure of fuel. The draught from the front door, if allowed to enter unchecked, blows all the heat up the chimney, and causes a fierce consumption of coal; this is arrested at once by *portières,* so I strongly advise them, not only because they look well, but because of the comfort and save of coal caused by adopting them.

There are several really inexpensive materials now-a-days which all make capital and artistic *portières:* first serge, which should always be lined if there is much draught; secondly, *carré* cloth, sold by Oetzmann for 2*s.* 11*d.* a yard, fifty inches wide. Five yards would be required for a door which opened into the room; for a door which opened out into the passage a width and a half would be sufficient, leaving the half width to go towards another curtain; thus for two doors seven and a half yards would be ample. Serge is 1*s.* 11½*d.* a yard, sometimes cheaper; it should be lined with Bolton sheeting at the same price and in the same colour, unless a more draped curtain is required, then the serge need not be lined: it falls in very graceful folds; and Colbourne, 82 Regent Street, W., has undoubtedly the

most artistic serges in London. His colours
are very good, and he keeps ball fringe to
match each colour he supplies—a great advantage to the tired or hurried shopper. I myself
am not fond of, neither do I recommend, the
ordinary cheap tapestry ; this is often as muddled and unpleasant in design as the builder's
papers alluded to in my first chapter. I therefore strongly advise either serge or *carré* cloth
for the *portières,* which should of course harmonize with whatever scheme of decoration
is selected by the tenant.

There are three ways of arranging *portières :*
if the door opens into the hall they must
simply hang straight down from one of Maple's
rods, which open and shut with the door ; if,
however, the door opens into the room, the
portière can be draped high on one side with
a cord and tassel, the first ring of the *portière*
being placed on the rod before it is fixed in
its place by the rose screw ; then all the other
rings are put on, and a cord is passed under
in such a way that it drapes the *portière* high
on one side ; a loop is made in the cord, which
is passed round the rose screw at the other

end,—this keeps the *portière* draped, and yet allows of its falling at once into place, should it be required to cover the door. A third way which is useful where there is very much draught is to drape the *portière* in this manner, and then on the opposite side of the door to where the draping is allowed to fall, to put a plain straight piece of material : half a width edged all round with ball fringe would be sufficient in an ordinary door; this arrangement has a specially good effect. This curtain should just, and only just, clear the floor, as indeed should all *portières*, or else they would soon become spoiled.

In selecting the decorations for the hall one must first consider the hall itself, and carefully study its capabilities and requirements, a dark narrow passage requiring perfectly different treatment to the wide light halls we would all have if we possibly could. But there is one thing to remember in all entrances, whether we dignify them by the name of hall or call them passages, and that is, that a real dado of some kind is a perfect necessity if we wish the place to be tidy and clean for any length of time, and I therefore cannot feel I am repeating myself too much if I insist that a paper dado is an impossibility, not only because it is hideously inartistic, but because it is of absolutely no use; far better, if you cannot afford matting, arras, or some good material, to paper simply from top to bottom with a paper that will take varnish well, although the expense of varnishing the paper will undoubtedly exceed the cost of a matting or arras dado.

Another thing to recollect is, that the colour of the front door should lead up to the colour to be found inside that door, that is to say, that if we select a red and white hall, the front door should be a much darker shade of red; if we select a yellow and white or a yellow and brown hall, the hall door should be nut-brown; and if we select a blue or green hall, the door should of course in a similar manner harmonize with the paper and paint which will be seen the moment the door is opened.

Here are therefore a few schemes for the decoration of small halls, which have all

been tried, and are all successful. In a dark
hall it would undoubtedly be wise to put
either a high arras dado of nut-brown, and
paper of Pither's yellow and white "berry" at
2s., as suggested before, or a red and white
paper called "Buttercup B," at 2s. 6d. a piece;
with this have a red and cream or else an
all cream matting dado, and paint with
Aspinall's "sealing-wax red," or his "stone."
With either of these decorations use Maple's
4d. a piece yellow and white ceiling paper,
and colour any cornice you may find cream;
and if you can afford it, have Pither's dark
blue Brussels stair-carpet at 4s. 7d. a yard,
or else Wallace's figured blue Burmese, or his
blue "Stella" at 3s. 11d.; this is Brussels
also, and nothing save pile or Brussels wears
for any length of time on the stairs. Even
this should have under-felt, and furthermore
should be protected from undue wear by
placing small pads, sold for the purpose by
Shoolbred, or any large furniture warehouse, on
the edge of the stairs; these in small houses
especially are apt to be extremely sharp and
rough, and unless really padded, cut out the

very strongest carpet in a most amazing way.
If the yellow and white and brown scheme is
accepted the front door should be "chocolate,"
and the hangings should be of old gold serge
or *carré* cloth; if the red and cream scheme
is chosen, the drapings can either be the same
blue as that used in the stair-carpet, or else
in the red of the paper; in both cases the
whole of the paint should be one even surface
of colour; the "treads" of the stairs only
being in Aspinall's white water paint, on
purpose for scrubbing, the white paint thus
relieving the expanse of colour, and making
the carpet look much nicer than it otherwise
would do. If the yellow and white "berry"
is considered too light even for a dark hall,
"Buttercup C" at 3s., all "mandarin" paint,
and a plain matting dado would make a very
charming hall; the ceiling could still have
Maple's 4d. a piece yellow and white paper,
the drapings could be of dull brown serge, and
the stair carpet could be Pither's golden-brown
Brussels. This hall is absolutely sure to be a
great success.

In a light hall I think blue is better than

any other colour, it is more uncommon and artistic-looking than any other shade; and here are two or three schemes. The first is Liberty's blue and silver tulip damasque paper at 2s. the piece, a dado of the plain matting sold by Treloar for 35s. the roll of forty yards, yellow and white ceiling paper, and either all ivory paint, or a blue which would be just two shades darker than the ground of the paper; have red serge hangings with this paper, and either Wallace's "red Stella" Brussels carpet at 3s. 11d., or Pither's red Brussels at 4s. 7d. Another absolutely safe blue hall is Pither's beautiful blue blossom at 1s. 6d. a piece, a dado of red and gold Japanese leather paper, and all dull red paint. "Cardinal No. 2" would be good with some Japanese papers, but if the painter can be trusted, the ground of the red should be matched exactly by him; if he cannot, it is best undoubtedly to send Mr. Aspinall a piece of the paper, and ask him to make an enamel paint to harmonize with that. "Scinde red" goes with some papers excellently, but whatever red is chosen, the last coat must be applied mixed with varnish; this not only dries the paint quickly, but gives the glossy look one always finds in enamel paint.

Another blue hall would be "Buttercup D," at 3s. the piece; with this the dado could be of plain greeny-blue serge, and the paint should be the greeny-blue of the leaf on the pattern; still yellow and white ceiling paper, and the red carpet—either the "Stella" or Pither's red carpets, looking better with blue walls than anything else possibly can.

If the hall is not only large and light, but very sunny and hot, one of Liberty's green and silver damasque papers would look extremely well, and give a cool atmosphere to the place — these are all 2s. a piece; a plain green matting dado would be very nice indeed; all dull green paint; a terra-cotta and white ceiling-paper, sold at 1s. a piece by J. and H. Land, 93 Cannon Street, E.C., would be the right paper to use with this decoration, and a terra-cotta carpet—Wallace has an excellent terra-cotta in a new design which would do excellently; the hangings should be terra-cotta or green to harmonize with the walls.

Of course there are endless combinations of colours to be made, and many other papers to be found, which would be quite as satisfactory as any of those I have named; but equally, of course, it would be impossible to speak of every pretty paper one sees; and I think I have given sufficient combinations here for any one to choose from; and if the colour of the papers please, and the design does not, recollect to keep to the colour,—which after all is the principal thing in decoration,—and do not allow yourselves to be talked out of the scheme; neither accept another paper which the builder declares is nearly the same—it must be absolutely the same, the " nearness " promised by the builder existing only in his own imagination, and resulting often, if not always, in a dreadful muddle and mixture of ideas and tints.

Personally I do not approve of the pseudo-Japanese and Oriental schemes of decoration of which English people have been so fond of late years; neither do I consider them suitable for the ordinary London or suburban house; and I equally object to the rags of muslin and flimsy draperies so much advocated by some few of my disciples; and I do not speak of this kind of adornment except to warn all would-be artistic folk against it, for unless they can go to a past master of the art, such as is Liberty, I can assure them their houses will be nothing save dismal failures. Let everything be bright, pretty, and suitable to the house, and I am quite sure there will be no need to pretend to be Japanese in order to have an artistic and delightful home.

I do most strongly here again advise no one to possess themselves of the ordinary hat-stand, which is such an eye-sore, and moreover such a temptation to thieves. In the first place, there is absolutely no reason, save the bad unreason of custom, why men's hats and coats should be left in the hall; but if they will have it so, let a corner in the hall be selected, and fix into that a V-shaped piece of wood with a bar straight across the front, put two V-shaped shelves one below the other for hats, and put some pegs on the wall itself for coats, and then in front, straight across the wooden bar, nail a couple of full curtains—I say a couple,

D

because they can be pushed aside, and the coats put in place. If a more elaborate affair is required, one can be bought of Wallace, who will also supply an oak buffet he has made to my design, or rather at my suggestion; which will take the place of the ordinary hall table. This should be decorated with large china jars, and hold an Imari basin for visiting-cards. These basins are about 2s. 6d. at Whiteley's, and have quite replaced the old-fashioned card-basket. A couple of chairs, one each side of the buffet, and a round brass stand for sticks and umbrellas would complete the furniture of an ordinary narrow hall, where the less one has in the way of "goods and chattels" the better; it only stuffs it up, and makes work for the housemaid.

On the buffet can be placed, beside the jars already recommended, a couple of the inexpensive art-pots sold for about 1s. 11d. each, and these can hold aspidistras. These are plants with broad striped leaves, of such long-suffering nature that they will exist almost without light, quite without sun; and with only the most moderate care will flourish splendidly.

Plants finish a house at once, and make up for
many shortcomings, and are sold so cheaply
now-a-days that few houses need be without
them.   I remember the days when plants
were only for the millionnaire ; now any one
who has a few pence can buy the most charming ferns and plants.   But not off the barrows
of the men in the street, please ; these unfor-
tunates have been dragged out of hot-houses,
and perambulated the streets in chilling winds,
sometimes for a day or two before finding a
purchaser ; what wonder when they do that
they die immediately, causing the purchaser
to declare that she will never waste her money
again.   But if she goes to a good florist, the
plants will be sent home at once and in good
order, and will repay her care by lasting some
weeks at all events, if not longer.

Of course gas is a great enemy to plants,
and gas we must have in the passages, at all
events until the dawning of that blessed day
which shall give us all the electric light ; but
until then our great care must be to select
really pretty and graceful lamps.   Undoubtedly
the best lamps for gas which have appeared

D 2

for years are the beaten iron ones one sees in most shop-windows; these are revivals of the beaten-iron trade, which was once a regular English art, and deserve every encouragement. Perhaps we may live to see it once more used for entrance-gates, grates, and the thousand and one ways of which evidences remain to us in some old places, and in some of the few remaining water-gates by the Thames; but in the meantime I strongly advise my readers to obtain gas-brackets, at Strode & Co.'s, 48 Osnaburgh Street, Regent's Park, and to see a centre lamp in beaten iron and bevelled glass sold by Verity in Regent Street for about 45s. This is an admirable lamp for an entrance, and cannot be improved upon, in my opinion.

An ordinary small house would require a hanging lamp in the front hall, and an arm on each landing; these arms or brackets should have the simple crinkled opal glasses sold by Whiteley for about 1s. 4½d. each. These are much nicer than any other kind, but the brackets used with these should have extra long burners; if these are not provided, the gas comes in the narrow part of the globe, and soon cracks it.

One more word, and then we will pass on to the furniture and decoration of the dining-room, and that is, never allow yourselves to be persuaded to put an aggravating little series of mats in each doorway; they always look ridiculous, and as they turn over every time a lady in a long dress passes them; and not unseldom follow her into the room entangled in her train; are as great a nuisance as they are useless and inartistic. If there should be a draught, put Slater's patent all round the door, or one of the draught excluders, which move up and down with the door. *Portières* hide any naked look, and of course the space by the door should be filled in with the linoleum, or whatever else is used to cover the hall-floor. Naturally a mat should be placed just at the front door, so that shoes may be duly wiped thereon; the best is one to be had of Treloar, in Ludgate Hill, in two shades of brown, in cocoa-nut fibre; these are usually made to fit a sunk space in the floor, and should have as companion, in a muddy district, not only a

scraper outside the door, but an ingenious
arrangement of brushes in a box, sold by
Shoolbred, and called, I think, an indoor
scraper ; this brushes off the worst of the mud
better than a mere mat can do.   It would be
well to stand this, and also the umbrella-stand,
on a small separate square of linoleum, as these
spots would be more tried than any other, and
these squares could be replaced with small cost
or trouble ; while worn or shabby patches in
the fabric itself, would necessitate fresh covering of the whole floor, for I do not think
linoleum could possibly be patched without
giving the whole house a most poverty-stricken
appearance.

Whatever other portion of the house is
allowed to be shabby, worn, or inartistic, I
would beg my readers never to relax their
attentions to the hall.   First impressions are
everything ; first impressions of the inhabitants
of a house are given by their windows, and
then by the hall ; and I therefore invariably
lay more stress on these two portions of the
house than any other, as few people will neg-
lect the rooms in which they live, because dirt,

untidiness, and ugliness there perpetually annoy them; while far too many forget the hall, and allow anything to do there, little thinking how loudly this speaks, when neglected, of the carelessness and untidiness of the careless and maybe slovenly owner.

CHAPTER III.

THE DINING-ROOM.

EVEN in quite small houses now-a-days there is generally some sort of a third sitting-room, and wherever this is the case, I do very strongly advise every one, to keep the dining-room simply for eating in; and I also often advise the smallest room of all being taken for this purpose. One does not require a great space for one's meals; while I think it is most unhealthy, it is certainly most disagreeable, to have to sit in the room where food has just been partaken of, and watch the remains being gradually removed, leaving behind them, alas! an aroma that can never be eliminated; dining-rooms which are lived in as well as eaten in, never losing the smell of food, especially in winter, when open windows are not always possible, and when one meal has scarcely been cleared away, before it is time to think about another one.

If, therefore, the dining-room can be kept just for food, the simpler it is furnished the better; but if we cannot, we must by aid of a window-seat and divers other devices make room for sitting comfortably. So it may be well, perhaps, to consider the room in its two aspects—of mere feeding place, and a combination of that and a chamber in which a good part of the day has to be spent.

Naturally before thinking of furniture the walls have to be decorated, and let me warn my readers specially against green as a colour here. I know no greens which light up even decently, and no colour is more depressing at night; therefore it should be avoided entirely for a dining-room, which should be the most cheerful room in the house. Personally I prefer red; it is always bright, always lights up excellently, and one never tires of it; and an excellent room, if one that is a little daring, can be made in a new house by using Pither's red and cream buttercup paper,

and staining all the new wood with the
malachite green stain sold by T. S. Jackson and Sons, 199 Borough ; the ceiling should
be papered with Pither's sage-green berry
paper, and all the furniture should be made
by Mr. Armitage, Stamford House, Altrincham, near Manchester, in his "artisan"
designs in stained green wood ; red corduroy
velveteen should be used for curtains, and
the floor should be covered with an excellent
green drugget sold by Burr and Elliott, in
Oxford Street, at 2s. a yard. This wears
splendidly, and on the surface thereof two
or three good Kurd rugs should be laid. The
table-cloth on the charming splay-legged table
sold by Mr. Armitage should be of dull green
serge, the exact shade of the green stain, and
edged round with woollen ball fringe. This
would be an inexpensive and really original
and charming room. Mr. Armitage would
send a price-list of his furniture illustrated
by sketches ; and if the house is not yet
furnished, I most strongly advise his mantle
and over-mantle in stained green wood, and
one of his "dressers," instead of the ordinary

ugly sideboard, which is as expensive as it is cumbersome, and absolutely inartistic in every way. The decorations and furniture in this room would be within the means of most of us, and would be infinitely superior to the cheap and ghastly "leather" suites which seem the ambition of so many, and which fall to pieces the moment they are tried in the very smallest degree.

In this dining-room all that would be required would be the table and ten chairs, and buffet. Oetzmann's church chairs with rush seats at 1s. 10d. each, stained green with the malachite stain, would be quite good enough, the rush seats being very soft and yielding to sit upon. The buffet or "dresser" stained green would be about £5 ; and I may mention that the ordinary kitchen dresser sold by Maple for about £4, stained green and carefully ornamented with cheap jars, basins, and plates, looks admirable in some houses ; and would be most effective where expense is a very great object. Of course the wooden handles should be eliminated, their places stopped up, and brass drop-handles put in

their stead. These drop-handles cost about
4¾d. each, and make a most wonderful differ-
ence in the appearance of the dresser; and if
very hard pressed, the dining-room, always the
most expensive room in the house, could be
decorated and furnished for something under
£20. In this case serge must be used instead
of the corduroy velveteen for curtains, serge
being 1s. 11½d., wide width, as against the
2s. 9d. of the velveteen, which is narrow, but
which would wear for a lifetime, and is most
artistic and excellent in every way.

A very charming dining-room can be procured by papering the walls with Pither's
excellent tapestry paper at 4s. 6d. the piece.
This paper is French, and in consequence is
French width. A piece and a half of this
paper covers the same wall space as does one
piece of English paper, and this should be
recollected when ordering it. With this paper
Aspinall's " imperial red " paint should be used,
and Maple's 4d. a piece yellow and white
ceiling paper; the floor should be stained for
about fourteen inches round with Jackson's
varnish stains; and one of the capital

Anglo-Indian carpets sold at Watford, Herts, by Pearkes and Sons, could be put down. These carpets require very careful choosing, but are very thick and serviceable, and being moderately cheap seem to me the best carpets I have ever seen for small dining-rooms, where there is a great amount of wear, and where expense is an undoubted object. Given this scheme of decoration, the curtains could be of Indian red serge, held back by wide bands of Colbourne's Gobelin tapestry ; this harmonizes splendidly with the paper, and furthermore makes excellent chair-covers ; it wears admirably, and looks far better in every way than ordinary leather. It is also an admirable material for re-covering old leather chairs, the frames of which do not seem to us to be worth having new leather seats and backs made to them. Wallace of 151 Curtain Road, E.C., has an excellent square chair he sells for dining-rooms, most inexpensively ; I think they are about 25s. each, and this shaped chair suits the tapestry style of covering better than any other ; the table-cloth should be imperial red serge. Let nothing persuade my readers to countenance the cheap and frightful figured tapestry cloths sold wholesale by most drapers, but let them adhere to plain serge, or felt, or cloth, affording themselves, if possible, one of the bordered plain cloths, made from a pattern supplied by me, to Messrs. Burnett and Co., King Street, Covent Garden; the centres of which are plain, and the borders are made from some contrasting hue; united to the plain centre by a gimp of both colours intermingled. These cloths should be edged with ball-fringe, and cannot, in my opinion, possibly be improved upon.

Another very original dining-room can be made by using no colours save brown and yellow together, but this can only be done properly in rather an expensive way; still, as it is quite novel, it may be worth speaking about, even in a pamphlet of merely inexpensive hints; for fashion changes so quickly, and also adapts expensive schemes of colouring to cheaper materials, that in fact, by the time this page is in print, the paper that now sell at 5s. 6d. a piece may be half that price; and a consignment of cheap Japanese leather

paper may have put in an appearance in the
market which may make the frieze within the
means of the poorest of us; so I will now
describe a scheme of colouring that is most
admirably adapted for use with Sheeraton or
Chippendale furniture, or in a house that is
really old; and not a pretence of sham oak,
and abominable attempts at looking the age
it will never live to attain, because of the
flimsiness of its construction. Nothing is
worse taste, my readers, than the shaky sham
oak, and venerable-looking rubbish, so many·
people put proudly into their suburban houses;
and fancy that at once the rooms look as if
they had been inhabited by them and their
forebears for generations.

There is a charming brown and gold paper
stamped on real brown paper for me by Essex
and Co., Albert Mansions, Victoria Street,
S.W., that should be the paper for a brown
and yellow room; all the paint should be a
dark soft *café-au-lait* brown, and this colour
should also be used on the frieze-rail; the
frieze itself should be of a brown and gold
Japanese leather paper, eighteen inches wide;

this can be made of a yard wide Japanese leather split to the proper width. This paper is about 1*s*. 6*d*. a yard, and the price of the frieze would be 9*d*. a yard. The ceiling paper should be yellow and white, and the window-curtains should be of russet brown serge, with yellow and white muslin underneath; the carpet should be Pither's golden-brown pile carpet, a square—this is 7*s*. 6*d*. the yard; the cloth should be russet brown with an old gold border; and the furniture, if old Chippendale cannot be picked up, should be walnut, after good plain designs from Wallace; with dull brown leather on the chairs, which should be a comfortable square shape, with a padded back.

I cannot impress upon my readers too often the absolute necessity of having comfortable, square, and padded backs to chairs in the dining-room; all too often, so long as these chairs look well, nothing more is thought about, and the unfortunate folk who have to sit on them all through a long stuffy dinner, not unseldom suffer a martyrdom they need not have endured for a moment, had any thoughts been given to the comfort, as well as the

appearance of the chairs. There is first and
foremost the square leather chair sold by
Wallace and Co. for about 45s., rather less
than more ; then comes an admirable chair,
either in saddle-bags or Gobelin tapestry from
the same warehouse at 26s., a most comfortable and pretty chair ; and finally the rush-
seated church chair of Oetzmann at 1s. 10d.
These require enamelling, and a long cushion
should be made for the backs, by cutting out
of a strong sheet of cardboard, the exact shape
and size of the back of the chair ; then on that
put a thick layer of cotton-wool or flock, or of
hair and flock mixed ; this should be covered
with sateen, which should also cover the cardboard behind. This species of pad is then
ready for its final covering, which can be of
ribbed velveteen, Shoolbred, 2s. 9d. a yard, of
Gobelin tapestry, or, in fact, of anything which
harmonizes with the room. At the top of
the cushion a stiff gauffered frill should be
put to finish it off, and the cushion should
be tied to the chair by four strings—two at
the top, two at the bottom. Of course the
chair should be aspinalled some art colour, or

E

else stained green, and thus a capital comfortable and artistic-looking chair can be had for
something under 5s.   Surely after that price
no one can complain that money stands in
the way of an artistic home.

And now let me here dwell upon one of my
pet fads or theories; and beg every one to join
with me, in a crusade against the blinds, and
fitted, heavy, and expensive poles, one finds
still in a great many, too many, small houses:
all fitted carpets, poles, and expensive gas-
fittings; acting as so many sheet-anchors to
bind us to a house, no matter how unhealthy,
disagreeable, and odious it may be, because
moving is made so expensive by our impedi-
menta, that we dare not contemplate it, unless
really driven to it by stress of circumstances;
but if we have square carpets, hanging lamps
in the rooms; and furthermore have some
slight brass rods, at a few pence a foot, to
replace roller-blinds, and cornices, and all
similar incumbrances; we can move with a
light heart, knowing that all our belongings
will fit in somewhere, and that we shall have
none of the waste, that makes moving, even

in these days, an impossibility, because we cannot afford it.

There are only about three kinds of windows to be found in the rooms of an ordinary villa: first the bow, with its three divisions and its wide sashes; then the ordinary flat window; and finally the French window, which often opens out into the street, and is in consequence the most tiresome window of all to manage. In the ordinary bow-window would be required six curtains of muslin, and four of any material one wishes to use; the curtains in the centre window should be frilled down each side, and should be hemmed top and bottom; the rods pass through these hems, and are fastened on the window-frame; *not the sash;* but the wooden frame which frames in the window, top and bottom; the stretched muslin reaches from the top of the window to the bottom, and can either cover the glass entirely by meeting in the centre; or can be eased away from the top to the bottom, and leave the window free for the view to be seen, according to the tastes of the owner, or to whether there were a view or not—views being, as a rule, conspicuous by their absence in the ordinary suburban house.

The side windows should be arranged in a similar manner ; and the thicker curtains, which are to draw at night, should depend from a three-quarter inch rod placed along the top of the window. A bow-window requires three of these rods, one straight along each division ; one wide curtain should be put down the wooden partition between the divisions in the centre, half on the centre, half on the side rod—this should draw half over the centre window, half over the side window ; and the side window should have a second narrower curtain at the end ; this would be wide enough to meet the other curtain, and so would cover the glass entirely. These curtains should only come just below the window-sill, should never be looped up, but should hang down in straight full folds ; and all curtains should be edged with ball-fringe or a frill—they should never have the hard untrimmed edge that spoils any window, and that I am glad to say is scarcely ever seen now.

A flat window is arranged simply like the

centre of the bow, with its two muslin curtains
and its two material ones; and a French
window must have the muslin on the window
itself, so that it opens and shuts with the
window; the heavier material should hang
straight down, and be about an inch on the
floor, not more—simply only to rather more
than touch the floor; these should be full
enough to draw completely over the window
when required, for nothing to my mind is
more ridiculous than a curtain so skimped
and miserable, one can see in a moment it
was never meant to draw: curtains should be
curtains, or should not exist at all. Why
should they? The best material for dining-
room curtains is undoubtedly corduroy velveteen; then comes a really good tapestry,
such as Colbourne's Gobelin tapestry; and
finally comes serge—the ever-useful artistic
serge at 1*s.* 11½*d.* a yard. *Carré* cloth sold by
Oetzmann at 2*s.* 11*d.* a yard is also an admirable material, and one that should undoubtedly
be inspected by the economical housewife; it
is far thicker than serge, and appears to me as
if it had a good deal more wear in it than that

most useful material has. When we think for
a moment of the curtains of our ancestors—the
wonderful crimson cloth which cost about 25*s.*
a yard, and was hideous, and all too swiftly a
prey to the all-devouring moth; of the odious
repps and moreens and the damasks, which
gave one the creeps whenever one touched the
wiry, "sleezy" surface, and the other stuffy
materials considered so handsome and so truly
"genteel"—we cannot, I feel, be too thankful
to the manufacturers who have produced for
us, materials that are a pleasure to look at; and
moreover are so inexpensive that we can replace them without a qualm when they become
shabby, or have absorbed too much of our
smoky atmosphere to be pleasant to live with.
Formerly new curtains only were possible once
in a lifetime; now we can have them every
few years, and not feel unduly extravagant
even then !

Up to the present we have only touched
upon the mere furniture that is absolutely
necessary in the most modest dining-room,
and have not suggested anything in the least
degree comfortable; first, because we wish to

impress on our readers the fact that the dining-
room should be what its name implies—a mere
salle-à-manger; and secondly, because ornaments are, after all, more than mere furniture
can be : to represent the private taste of the
individual, more than anything else. Still, as
many may be forced to inhabit their dining-
rooms, we will give a few suggestions of what
can be done in the way of comfort before
passing on to consider the other rooms.

In the first place, a seat round the bow-
window is a most useful and charming possession, and can be made at home quite easily if
the husband has the smallest idea of carpentering, or the wife of using her needle; for all
that is required is a wooden frame about fourteen inches high, and about eighteen broad;
this has eight legs—four in front, four behind,
and two of these legs come in each angle, and
two at each end of the seat. The top is made
by nailing a stair-drill tightly and carefully
along the top, and a few straps of webbing
underneath also give great assistance; then
a full flounce of any material is hung on nails
by rings along the front and sides, and a

cushion in three divisions is placed along the top of the seat. This cushion should be stuffed with flock and a little wool, and should be covered in the same material of which the flounce is composed. If the seat is high enough for a back this can be made from three flat cushions hung on the wall with rings and nails ; these should be edged with a frill. A full sketch of this window is given in *From Kitchen to Garret*, and from this any amateur carpenter could easily make himself a luxurious seat, where, if he be a smoker, he can smoke after dinner comfortably, or where his wife can sit and sew or read, should she have no third room in which to spend her days.

In this case a couple of arm-chairs should be added to the slender plenishing of the little room ; these cannot be better, in my mind, than the excellent saddle-bag chairs sold by Wallace for £6 6*s.* the two—one chair for a gentleman, the other for a lady ; these look very handsome and are very comfortable, and are less expensive than any other kind I have ever come across. Each chair should have a footstool ; and footstools should also not be forgotten for underneath the dining-table : nothing is worse to some people than to have to sit through a long meal with their feet dangling direfully in mid-air, being just unable to reach the ground.

A writing-table is a *sine quæ non* in a room that has to do double duty; for notes and letters must be written, and it is not always convenient to do this on the larger table, where meals may be laid, and the cloth runs the risk of being inked ; and with a little care a carpenter could be found to make a species of wooden table with drawers for about £2 10s. The drawers should be deep, and capable of holding a good store of paper and odds and ends generally. The table could be aspinalled, or stained green, and brass drop-handles should be put where the ordinary handles are placed ; then the top should be covered with Japanese leather paper—this looks far better than ordinary cheap leather, and can be replaced for a few shillings as soon as it becomes inked or shabby. Shabby leather, like shabby leather chairs, must always be adhered to, because of the fearful expense

of re-covering with the same material, another
reason for using cheap materials ; for if we do,
we need never be really shabby : we can always
look neat and nice.

The decoration of the walls is a thing that
ought to occupy the mind of a small house-
holder rather more than it does at present,
especially now one can purchase autotypes and
photographs so very, very cheaply and so
very easily.   Over and over again I have been
told, " If I cannot have really good pictures
I will have none at all."   Now what con-
stitutes a good picture, I wonder ?   A collection of Millais, and of the Royal Academicians,
or of the old masters is out of the question
for all moderate means.   Much less known
of artists are equally so, for one must be
unknown of indeed if one cannot get £20 for
a small picture, and had better take to anything save art under these melancholy circumstances ; so there is nothing left for us but
autotypes, which are unfading, and being
accurate copies of the pictures, are as good art
as the picture itself ; and let me impress upon
all who are about to furnish to retain some

money for pictures, without which, try how one will, no room can ever be furnished or seem homelike.

Then even in the dining-room there must always be flowers and plants ; a big fern in a cheap art pot must of course be in the centre of the table, and a stand of flowers in the room is also a great assistance to making the room look finished and pretty ; and of course a few cut flowers should be on the mantel-piece, which should have a clock of some kind, a couple of holders for spills, and a couple of candlesticks ; the rest of the ornaments can be Kaga or Imari ware, or that delightful blue and white china which Whiteley sells so very very cheaply, and which Liberty, and Hewett and Co of the Baker Street Bazaar were the first to introduce into England, a feat for which they should be rewarded greatly by all who really care for the decoration of their homes.

If the mantelpiece has the simple wooden mantel and over-mantel of which we spoke before, nothing save judiciously chosen orna-ments should be placed upon the shelf ; but

if the unlucky tenant finds himself provided
with what house-agents term a "statuary
marble mantelpiece," let him not be deluded
into arranging elaborate and extremely dirty
wisps of draperies about it, let him accept
the inevitable, after first trying to be allowed to paint it the exact shade of the
rest of the woodwork. If, however, he is not
allowed to do this; and even if he is; he
should content himself with an admirable
drapery made at the Guild, 11 Kensington
Square, W., for about 30s. This hides a good
part of the marble, can be shaken daily if
desired, and breaks the line between the mantel
and over-mantel most satisfactorily, the while
it gives quite sufficient idea of drapery, without being a dust-trap merely, as are so many
of the so-called fire-place decorations. The
drapery is made, I may inform those of my
readers who would like to make it at home,
by taking a straight piece of material, about
twenty-seven inches wide and twenty-four
inches longer than the mantelpiece itself;—the
best material is Bokhara plush, the next best
corduroy velveteen;—the ends and front should

have either a cord or ball-fringe run on ; at
each end there should be a tassel, and as the
corners show, they should be lined with sateen
either in a contrast or the same colour exactly.
Then the drapery is ready, and it is put on,
the untrimmed edge against the wall, in such
a way that twelve inches hang over at each
end of the mantelpiece, and a wide straight
piece hangs all along the mantelpiece itself.
Can anything be simpler ? and yet hardly
any one I know has been able to make it
without seeing a specimen ; why I can't for
the life of me make out.

The hints for a dining-room would certainly
not be complete without a few words respect-
ing the arrangement of the table at meals,
and ideas for the decoration thereof, for
recollect ! no plea of poverty ever excuses a
woman, in possession of all her faculties, and
of good health, from keeping her table as
fresh and clean and appetizing to look at, as
if she had a butler and half a dozen footmen,
for with a linen-press and moderate care a
table-cloth can be kept fresh and nice. She
can fold it, aye, and wash and iron it herself

without much trouble ; and she can also keep the glass, china, and silver in spotless purity with her own hands ; rather than allow her table to be slovenly, or untidy-looking in the smallest possible degree ; and furthermore, I do strongly advise all girls to learn to mark their table-linen with well-designed monograms as the Germans do. This gives a *cachet* at once to the linen, and is no more trouble than the miserable daubs of painting and useless fancy-work that occupy the minds and fingers of so many middle-class women, and prevent them ever learning anything of the finer portion of household work.

An amount of silver should never be used where there is no time to keep it in order ; of course spoons and forks must be used, but charming china salt-cellars and arrangements for pepper and mustard, replace now-a-days the gruesome cruet-stand that is never seen now in a house that has the smallest pretensions to being artistic, or even moderately pretty ; while plain glass and china can be had quite easily, and always look well if kept bright and clean.

A simple style of decoration for every-day
use is a wide low brass or china pot planted
with bushy ferns; four small ferns in blue
and white pots can stand at each side, with
a single blue and white Japanese jar between
each pot; these would hold a single flower
and morsel of fern, and be four in number.
The total cost is infinitesimal in these days,
and at once there is a centre for the table
which is quite enough, and would last weeks
as far as the ferns are concerned, at an
absurd amount of expenditure both of time
and money.

CHAPTER IV.

DRAWING-ROOMS.

It is rather more difficult to furnish the room set apart for "company" in a small house than any other.

In the first place, the very name "drawing-room" sounds so pretentious and gorgeous, that naturally we all hanker after furniture which shall in some measure accord with the name; but I unhesitatingly state, that owners of a small house with the orthodox two rooms— one each side of the passage called by courtesy hall—would be much wiser if they dropped the more pretentious name, and contented themselves with the modest "parlour," which may mean anything; for is not one of society's great ladies content to name one of her rooms the "Iris parlour"? and therefore we cannot be accused of vulgarity and old-fashionedness if we elect to follow her august example. And I am sure, if the reader of these "inexpensive hints" is wise, she will content herself with a charming simple parlour, and will not hanker after the temple of the graces; which, even in these artistic days, is all too often set aside for use when only strangers are present, and in consequence chills to the bone any who are venturesome enough to enter within its scarcely used portals.

The orthodox small room, with its stiff bow-window, its green and gold paper; all too often accentuated and made doubly hideous by a green and gold paper dado in squares; with a paper border to simulate a rail, its huge and vulgar marble mantelpiece (that emblem of gentility!) and coloured cornice, is all too well known to all of us to need any farther description; and as many cannot afford to entirely re-paper and paint at their own expense, and as unfortunately it generally happens that the uglier a paper is, the more the landlord assures his tenant that it is far too good to remove; I will turn my attention first to telling my

F

readers how best to mitigate the horrors of
such a room, should they find themselves
unable to alter the paper; though as this can
generally be done for about £2, I trust that
the paper may be removed as soon as possible,
and replaced by one of Pither's simple, inexpensive, and charming papers; all of which
may be put up safely, as they are all successful
in colour and design, which is more than can
be said for a great many papers.

But given the green and gold room, and this
is how I should proceed to tackle it.   I should
insist on the cornice being colour-washed cream,
and the ceiling should be papered with a cream
and pink ceiling paper.   This costs at the rate
of 1*s*. a piece, and 1*s*. a piece is also the orthodox
charge for hanging it.   This will alter the
room immensely; and then if the paint is as
usual picked out, or striped in various hues, as
is the case almost invariably in similar rooms,
Aspinall should be called into use, and one
coat of soft gray-green should be given to
the paint.   This if done by the amateur himself would cost about 5*s*., and no one who has
not seen and contrasted the room as it appears

now, with how it looked when the stripes and pickings out were left, in their pristine hideousness, can understand in the least how these simple touches redeem what was once a vulgar commonplace room, and make it almost artistic without farther trouble.

The door need not be painted, for if one of Maple's rods, which open and shut with the door, be procured, and an inexpensive material used for a *portière* be hung from that; the door is completely hidden, and the entire room receives an air of comfort from the *portière* which is sadly lacking in the ordinary square room of the period. The *portière* could be made from Oetzmann's excellent *carré* cloth, at 2*s*. 11*d*. a yard in terra-cotta, and this should have the edges sewn over with long stitches in coarse art-green crewels. There should be one long stitch, the next should be shorter, the third shorter still, the fourth should be the length of the second, the fifth of the first; and this arrangement should be repeated all round the bottom and up both sides. Of course a bold design of green leaves and darker terra-cotta flowers would much improve the look of the *portière*, and a good worker could soon transform the two yards and a quarter of plain cloth into a thing of beauty with very little trouble if she set to work steadily, and used coarse crewels and a good design. If it can be managed, a good way of covering the greater part of the wall would be to put round it, about five feet from the ground, an iron rod such as pictures are hung from; this should be painted green like the rest of the paint, and from this should be hung all round the room a closely draped curtain of dark green art serge, or of thin Liberty silk, or even of printed linen at $9\frac{3}{4}d$. a yard. Of course this would cost a great deal more than papering the room, but the curtains could be removed at any moment, and they and the rods would always be tenant's property; while what we spend on papering would at once be lost, and could never be reclaimed. The curtain idea should therefore commend itself to some of my readers who do not care so much what they spend, if they know it always remains their own property, and that they can remove it when they go.

I saw a very clever adaptation of this curtain theory the other day, where the curtain was not the same height all round the room. For about six feet, say, it ran along on straight about eight feet from the floor, then it dropped for about three feet to five feet from the floor, leaving a square space, covered in this especial chamber in Japanese leather paper, which material covered all the space above the hangings, but which in an ordinary room could be filled either with a favourite picture, a round mirror, a group of candles, a hanging lamp, or even a square bracket to hold flowers and china. But if the walls must be let alone, I should advise, at any rate, a real wooden-rail above the paper dado, painted the same colour as the rest of the paint, and that as many pictures as possible can be hung both on the dado itself and immediately above the offending thing itself.

The mantelpiece should be next dealt with. It should be enamelled green all over the marble with Aspinall's enamel, and I should do this without telling any one. All the paint comes off at once with Carson's " Detergent,"

you can try a corner first before painting the
whole surface; and then on the shelf should be
placed one of the simple "guild" draperies,
which can be bought complete at the rooms of
the Workers' Guild, 11 Kensington Square,
W., for about 30s. These draperies are so
extremely simple, however, that any one could
make it herself without any trouble at all.
She has nothing to do but take a piece of any
material, twenty-seven inches wide, and about
twenty-four inches longer than the mantelpiece
itself; up each end and along the front of the
piece of material should be sewn a silk cord of
the same colour as the material; each corner
should be lined on the cross with a thin satin
a shade or two lighter than the material itself,
and to each front corner should be sewn a light
silk tassel, or a group of small pom-poms.
The drapery is now absolutely finished, and
is put on, the untrimmed edge against the
wall; the hemmed edge hangs over the shelf,
and should be quite fourteen inches in depth
from the edge of the shelf; the corners drape
themselves. And this is undoubtedly the only
drapery which should ever be allowed near a

fire-place, being easily removed, as there is absolutely no fixing. It can be shaken daily, and it runs small risk of catching fire, and it is neither dangerous nor stuffy, as far too many so-called draperies are at present. In the green hues to which our thoughts have been directed, the drapery should be in the shade of terra-cotta known as shrimp-pink, which said colour should pervade the room, and in some measure redeem it from the dullness inseparable from any scheme of colour which includes very much green; a restful colour enough, but one that can never be considered, or made to look, cheerful, strive as one may. The carpet should be Wallace's admirable "green lily" carpet; this is 3s. 9d. the yard, wide width. It should be put down over a carpet felt-edged with a fringe, and should be square. The carpet being surrounded by either staining or terra-cotta Indian matting, whichever is chosen, should not fit in the bow; where also a rug in some foreign make should be laid; and where the same arrangement both for seat and curtains which I have described while writing about the dining-room should likewise be carried out.

The curtains should either be terra-cotta
and green cretonne,—Helbronner, 300 Oxford
Street, has a beauty at 1s. 8d. a yard, which
would make any room look artistic,—or else
of terra-cotta damask from Colbourne, 82
Regent Street, at 2s. 11d. a yard, or of the
carré cloth at 2s. 11d., or in the humble serge
at 1s. 11d. The cretonne curtains should be
lined with Burnett's lining at 7d. a yard in
dark green, and should be edged, as should
also the other materials, with a ball-binding at
$6\frac{3}{4}d$. a yard, sold by Colbourne; this finishes
off the edge of the curtains nicely, and is no
trouble to make. The white curtains should
either be of Wallace's "*guipure vitrage*," or
else of Kay's India muslin; the former is
$10\frac{1}{2}d$. a yard, but requires no making, simply
hemming top and bottom, the rods passing
through these hems. The India muslin is
$2\frac{1}{2}d$. a yard; cheaper if a large quantity be
bought; but that must be edged with frills,
and as these must be hemmed by hand,—the
machine pulls the muslin out of shape in some
curious manner,—there is a good deal of work
in a pair of curtains! Nothing looks nicer

than full-frilled curtains of Kay's India muslin, and it is worth a little trouble to obtain the satisfactory result that is arrived at in the front of a house, the windows of which are entirely draped round in the manner I am never tired of advocating. The rods for the muslin should be slighter than those for the thicker curtains, and should be fastened on the window-frame, not on the sashes ; the thicker rods are placed above the window only, and the curtains hang down from them straight, and are not looped ; they can be drawn swiftly and easily over the window at night, or to obscure the sunshine, and are therefore quite sufficient for a window ; which, arranged like this, cannot possibly need blinds of any sort or description, except in an extremely sunny situation. In this case outside blinds are necessary, as the great heat is caused by the sun striking on the glass itself, which naturally is not obviated in the least by the use of an inside blind.

The room would now be ready for furnishing, and the manner in which that is done must depend entirely on what we have to spend. The good saddle-bag arm-chairs can be had for

about £6 6s. the two from Wallace in the
Curtain Road, who will also supply a most
artistic cabinet for about £7. Small tables
cost in walnut from 17s. 6d. upwards; a
couple of these, and a large one at about
£2 2s., a card-table, and about four rush-
seated chairs, and two low basket-chairs upholstered in pretty cretonne would be quite
enough furniture to begin with, more especially
if the bow-window be fitted with a seat, and
the orthodox piano should be forthcoming.

Very often there are recesses by the side of
the fireplace, and should this be the case, one
would be most useful filled in with Godfrey
Giles' cosy corner ; this can be removed at will
at any time, and comes to about £7 17s. 6d. ;
while the other could have shelves for books,
hanging a curtain down the centre to break
the straight line, and edging the shelves with
two and a half inch frills of the same material
at that used for the curtain. Ordinary velveteen, or Shoolbred's ribbed corduroy velveteen
is a capital material. A good effect is also
obtained by breaking up the line of shelf by
tiny corners and arches of Moorish fretwork ;

this can be bought of Holroyd and Barker in
Oxford Street; and if this is used, and tiny
curtains here and there of Liberty silk added,
the recess becomes really a charming corner;
the top of which serves as an admirable home
for china and photographs, and odds and ends
generally; above the shelves should be hung
a couple of photographs or autotypes; and a
wide open Spanish fan on one side, and a
large Imari plate on the other; would cover
a good space here of the obnoxious wall
papers! Above the cosy corner side should be
hung a round mirror, and above the seat itself,
from the ceiling, should depend a lamp; the
corner would thus be a warm nook for winter
reading, more especially if a small screen
stood at the end of the seat, between the end
and the window. Screens are extremely cheap
now-a-days, and, judiciously used, add immensely to the appearance of a room, no
matter its size. I say judiciously, for I have
heard of an ignoramus who, by way of making
an artistic improvement in her commonplace room, erected a series of screens there,
each concealing a table and chair, in such

a manner that her chamber resembled nothing so much as a small restaurant. She had heard screens were being much used, and was evidently determined to be well in advance of the fashion, although she did live in the country !

But without emulating this lady we can have the screens, even in a little room : one at the end of the cosy corner, the other the side of the door opposite to that on which the door opens. This gives an idea of space which is really marvellous ; but if this is objected to, the screen is very often useful at the side of the piano ; which should if possible be turned out from the wall in such a way that the performer faces the room, and does not, as was the fashion for so many years, sing all her songs into the wall ; in a manner which must have tried a good singer very much indeed. Sometimes a piano looks well placed with one end against the wall in the recess of which I was writing just now, and the other straight out into the room. In this case, and indeed in any case where the back of the piano is exposed, the hideous baize covering should be hidden in some way or the other. Japanese leather does sometimes, and some people fit in a square of American leather, and paint a device on that; but the simplest, and in my opinion by far the best way is to obtain one of Shoolbred's piano rods; these are fastened on just below where the piano opens, and from these should be hung a simple full curtain of some decorative material,—Wallace's "daisy brocade" is as cheap and effective as most people would care for,—in such a manner that the back of the piano is completely hidden. Along the top should be laid a piece of Japanese embroidery, and a photograph frame in brocade; a low Salviati cup for flowers, and one or two ornaments would be placed there; but these should be capable of being removed in a moment should we be either very musical ourselves, or number musical enthusiasts among our friends; for then the lid of the piano has to be opened, and our ornaments must not be in the way should this occur. Sometimes a sofa can go straight along the back of the piano, or else the writing-table, and either a screen can be put at one end, or a tall stand to

hold a palm in an art pot; not, however, one
of those very common painted wood pot-stands
seen in every shop-window, but one that is
really good and gracefully designed, or else it
is much better not to have anything of the
kind at all. Cheap painted odds and ends
have had their day, and are to be eschewed by
all who really require an artistic home. The
chair backs should be simply folded over, so
that both ends show, and should always be the
embroidered Turkish antimacassars sold by
Stephens, 326 Regent Street, or Liberty, or
Debenham and Freebody. One can generally
buy very good specimens at about 3s. 6d. each,
but one must look about for these articles.
Sometimes Liberty has beauties at 3s. 6d., and
again one may go there and find nothing one
likes under 12s. I fancy it depends, like
matting and Japanese leather paper, on the
shipments and consignments; therefore it
behoves one not to make one's purchases in a
hurry; they are to be had at 3s. 6d., but if
not to-day they certainly will to-morrow, or at
latest next week.

Each small table should have its square loose

cloth edged with ball-fringe; in the green room these cloths may be of terra-cotta, sage green, and turquoise blue serge, or else of damasks in similar colouring. The material would depend naturally on what one could afford; but the cloths should be square, and large enough to hang gracefully at the corners. And as many plants and flowers must be brought and placed about the room as one has time and money for—large palms and the ever-useful aspidistras, living for years if properly tended in a gas-less atmosphere, and being in consequence far cheaper than the flowering plants that only live a few days at most, and have then to be thrown away.

Before I conclude the chapter on the drawing-room, I will give one or two schemes of colouring for those who are lucky enough to be able to choose their own. For those who are able to keep their drawing-room simply for evening use, there is no colour better, I am convinced more and more, than a clear yellow and white scheme of colour; it lights up magnificently, and is always cheerful. This in a small room can be obtained inexpensively by

using Pither's yellow and white special berry
paper, and a plain yellow frieze in a deeper
shade, or else a frieze of Essex & Co.'s, Albert
Mansions, Victoria Street, yellow Othmar paper.
The curtains and chair-covers should be of some
clear yellow and white material ; like Collinson
and Lock's "47" cretonne, Graham and
Biddle's "carnation" or "double poppy" ; and
the carpet should be Pither's dull red or dull
blue Brussels at 4s. 7d., or his pile at 7s. 9d., or
else Wallace's "lily" at 3s. 9d., according to
the price to be given. All the paint should
be ivory, while the ceiling paper should be
yellow and white, the cornice being coloured
cream simply, as should all cornices wherever
they may happen to be placed. Touches of
warm colour, such as red and blue, may be
given in the table-cloths, china, and flowers,
but the scheme of the room should be yellow
and white, and will be found when lighted up
to be most satisfactory. By the way, all
lighting must be done by good copper lamps ;
beauties can be found at W. A. S. Benson and
Co.'s, New Bond Street, W., for £2 12s. 6d.
each. Two would be required in the ordinary

small room, and they would soon save their cost in the manner in which the plants would live, and the room itself remain clean ; gas kills one's flowers, and very soon spoils all one's pretty dainty surroundings.

If the drawing-room is a day as well as a night room, it is best to make it a blue "arrangement." Mr. Smee sells an admirable paper the right shade of blue at 4s. the piece, of which one never tires, and with this all blue paint should be used : Aspinall's electric turquoise is a beautiful shade. The ceiling should be yellow and white, the curtains and furniture yellow ; and the floor should be covered either with matting and rugs, or else by a square of the blue "lily" carpet, or as much richer a carpet in the same shades of blue as the "lily" as funds will allow, and this room will be a great success. I do not, by the way, speak much of dados and friezes, as these are hints for folks who have not very much money to spend, but this last room would naturally be much improved by a broad frieze, either of plain gold Japanese paper, or else of dark blue American leather,

G

on which different coloured roses could be painted. These rose-friezes are of course costly, being about 7s. 6d. a yard, but they can be removed like a picture can, and are as much a tenant's property as are his pictures. In this case care must be taken to paper behind them with a plain paper, so that the room will look all right when it is moved.

I most strongly advise all my readers to make a stand with the landlord on the subject of grates. The slow combustion grate saves its own cost in a very few weeks, and should therefore be in every house, and should be asked for by every tenant; who should, moreover, make special request for the simple and graceful wooden mantles and over-mantles in plain deal for painting to match the rest of the room. These cost one-third of the bright steel and gorgeous marble abominations which die such lingering deaths, and are therefore to be commended heartily for more reasons than one; and I do hope to stir up somehow a revolt on the part of tenants, generally; over the petty tyrannies landlords are so fond of exercising, in the shape of these wasteful grates and ugly mantelpieces; to say nothing of the wretched papers spoken of before; and which all contrive so successfully to prevent a cheap house from ever becoming an artistic home. To be artistic these small details must be attended to, and more is done for the appearance of a room by a plain mantle and over-mantle *en suite*, and a tiled stove, than by almost any amount of expensive decoration; the tiled hearth, and tiled curb fender, which should accompany this style of decoration, making the work of the servant who has to clean the grate, about one-third as heavy as it used to be, in the days of much blacklead and more bright steel.

This chapter on drawing-rooms would not be complete without just one word on the subject of the floral room, which is so charming, especially in the country. Here the wall paper should match the cretonne; a cretonne dado should run round the room, fastened by the dado rail, which should be screwed on to enable the cretonne to be removed for washing purposes; the wood-work should either be enamelled ivory or stained "malachite green";

all the furniture should be in cretonne covers,
edged with gauffered frills on the small chairs ;
and flounces down to the ground in the case
of sofas and large arm-chairs ; the carpet should
either be sage green in the "lily" colours, or
else the warm terra-cotta red *in pile* that Wallace and Pither both sell in the right shades ;
and one kind of cretonne should be used for
all, curtains included.   Godfrey Giles has useful papers and cretonnes to match ; and the
"silk rose," the "iris," and "No. 6" may all
be depended on to work out in a most satisfactory manner.

A drawing-room can be furnished really
nicely for about £40 ; it should not be
called a drawing-room under that sum.   It
can be furnished simply for about £25, but
the larger sum is none too large really, while
of course any amount could be spent ; but
whatever is purchased, I must strongly advise my readers to keep some money in hand,
to be spent after the house has been arranged,
and lived in some few weeks ; for it is
utterly impossible to really furnish a house
artistically and completely ; until it has been

learned, and its wants discovered. It would be most unwise for any bride and bridegroom to furnish like this, and spend *all* their money before they are married. Presents drop in wonderfully at the last, and they may find themselves possessed of all the ornaments, and half the furniture for their drawing-room ; after they have spent money they would have been glad to spend elsewhere, on the very things that now come pouring in. So again I utter my favourite word of warning—do not be in a hurry, and only buy absolutely necessary furniture ; until the house has been lived in by you, and in a measure understood by you too !

CHAPTER V.

THE BEDROOMS.

THE advance that has been made during the last few years in the twin arts of house furnishing and house decorating is, I think, far more perceptible in our bed-chambers than in any other rooms in the house. Even in the darkest days—the days of green reps, four-post bedsteads, fitted carpets, moreen hangings, and all other monstrosities of a like nature—there was always some sort of struggle made to have a pretty drawing and handsome dining-room; but the poor up-stairs portion of the house was all too often, either a refuge for the destitute, in the shape of half-worn carpets, and shakily constituted drawing-room chairs; or else a dark and unwholesome collection, of anything that was tasteless, unhealthy, and detestable; while no thought nor care, and absolutely not an atom of artistic consideration, were given to the bedroom, where, after all, a considerable portion of our lives, and not always the pleasantest, has to be passed.

A bedroom, in my opinion, cannot possibly be too bright, light, and cheerful. It should never be over-burdened with furniture, and should, above all, never have very much in it, or, in fact, anything that cannot be continuously moved, to allow of all the accumulations of dust being removed at least once a week. Very heavy wardrobes and curtained beds are to be deprecated, as indeed is anything that is in the least degree stuffy, or likely either to collect dust or prevent the free circulation of air. I am no great advocate for darkened rooms, except for small children, and am entirely against the dreary blinds and heavily curtained and closed windows one finds even now constantly in houses; and I should like to contrast for a few moments one's sensations after a night spent in one of those dark and closed rooms, to that where both light and air are allowed to come. And by light I do not

mean the untempered glare of a May sun, but
the light that filters through the lined cretonne
curtain; as compared to the heavy darkness
caused by Venetian blinds, supplemented by a
rep, or serge, or moreen curtain.   In the light
and airy room getting up is no penance : one
is refreshed by one's night's rest, and is absolutely ready for the day's work; which the
happy sunshine outside seems to invite one
to ; in the other a dreary sense of the useless-
ness of doing to-day, what must be done again
in due course when to-morrow comes, seizes
one ; the darkness invites one to more slumber
and more sleep; and, in fact, what is a
pleasurable duty in the one case, becomes a
terrible toil in the other ; which, moreover,
incapacitates one almost entirely from doing
anything which we ought to do with a cheerful
and light heart.

Moreover, the style of furniture and decoration that I am about to advocate is much less
expensive than the ordinary run of furniture,
and therefore should undoubtedly recommend
itself to my readers ; while I cannot too often
repeat the statement, that no one can take too

much pains about their house, no one can take
too much thought or trouble over a place where
the rest of life will most probably be spent; or
on things which should last our lives, even
if we cannot hand them on, in the good old-
fashioned way, to our children and grand-
children.

Furniture, be it understood, only, for
carpets, curtains, papers, and paint should be
continually renewed, which is why I most
strongly advocate cheap hangings and decorations. It is so much healthier to get rid of
the dust of ages, as represented by a venerable
carpet and dust-worn curtains, than to clean
and sweep and shake them; of course I mean
after using them for a decent space of time;
while furniture is always capable of being
cleaned, and therefore should last longer than
it seems to be able to do in these days of
shoddy and universal cheapness. I therefore
advocate good wooden furniture being bought,
from a firm like Wallace in the Curtain Road,
or from Hampton in Pall Mall East, or from
Smee in 89 Finsbury Pavement: all these
firms are absolutely to be trusted for excellent

workmanship, and will honestly replace any article that warps or splits from unseasoned wood ; while other large firms have not only the lack of conscience to send out green wood, which flies, like butter before the sun, the moment it is exposed to the smallest heat, but often are exceedingly rude when asked to replace the thing ruined by their carelessness for another. I long to name names, but a wholesome fear of an action for libel prevents my doing this ; still I can state, and state positively, that all the firms named here have been tried by me, and have in every case proved to be most satisfactory and most anxious to please, and that too in the days when I could not have recommended them to a soul : as regards Smee and Hampton ; I have only known of and tried Wallace's furniture since I wrote *From Kitchen to Garret*, and my articles in the *Ladies' Pictorial*.

It is no use to buy rubbish ; if this is done we can never stop buying, for the things fall to pieces almost before they are put in their places, and are a constant source of worry and expense. As a rule, a bedroom can be fur-

nished cheaply and prettily for about twenty
pounds, and I do not advise any one to
attempt to do it for less, though of course it
can be done perfectly well, but not with good
furniture, or furniture that would be a pleasure
to look at; and even on this sum the furniture
would not be very large or imposing. Wallace's "Lonsdale suite No. 3," at £10 5s., is a
really pretty suite, and comprises 3 feet 6 in.
wardrobe, toilet table fitted with glass and
four drawers, excellent washing-stand with
the high-tiled back and deep cupboard that
no washing-stand should lack; and a couple of
chairs, leaving just under £10 more for the
carpet, bed and bedding, and the curtains, etc.
With this suite, which can be had either in ash,
walnut, or mahogany, and which has pretty
brass handles and bevelled glass both in the
wardrobe and toilet-table, I should advise
a square carpet of the "red lily" pattern
sold by Wallace—this for a small room would
come to about £4, an iron and brass bedstead
and bedding would be another £4, leaving
£1 15s. for cretonne and muslin curtains,
which would be ample, and leave a few shil-

lings for something else ; and no bedroom
should be really furnished under that sum,
while of course as much more could be spent
as my readers have at their disposal, Wallace's
No. 2 suite at £18 18*s*. and his No. 1 at
£21 10*s*. being especially artistic and good in
design.

There are several small things about bedroom furniture which should always be
remembered. In the first place, the bed should
be absolutely unencumbered by any drapery
at all ; it should be a plain metal bed ; brass
if it can in any way be afforded, but if not
the iron bedstead should be enamelled an art
colour ; I myself prefer ivory ; though naturally any brass that might be about the bed
should not be touched ; only the black iron
should be enamelled, and should be undertaken
by the firm of whom the bedstead is purchased.
I think, by the way, Japanned is the proper
title ; enamelling would hardly answer in this
special case, as a bed is so very much and continually moved about. Allow no valances, no
trimmings of any kind, and no curtains ; have
an Excelsior chain mattress, and a good hair

mattress over that, four pillows and a bolster, and you will have an absolutely hygienic couch, and one that is easily cleaned and disinfected should you be so unfortunate as to be laid up with scarlet fever, small-pox, or any other equally pleasing disease.

The bed should have, tied over the chain mattress by tapes at the four corners, a strong square of crash : this can be sent to the wash once or twice a year ; the hair mattress should have its edges protected by a strip of brown holland, which should fold over underneath and above the mattress for about twelve inches this could always be removed to be washed, and would prevent a mattress being soiled in the tiresome way it all too often is by the dirty aprons of the maids ; while new pillows should also be put in pillow covers before the ordinary cases go on, or else the ticks will always be going to be cleaned, and the feathers will have to be taken out and picked over, in a manner that is as wasteful as it is undoubtedly tiresome.

Windows vary so much in shape and size that only mere outlines can be given of the

way to manage them; but on no account
should the wretched little half-way curtains of
which English people are so fond be allowed.
Nothing spoils the appearance of a house like
these do, and nothing is more absolutely tasteless and useless. In the first place, these
half-way abortions are always fixed on the
window sash, and go up and down whenever
the window is opened; thus leaving the whole
room and the inhabitants thereof exposed to
the public gaze. No one in a room with these
blinds can dress with the window open; and,
in fact, I never can see the reason why they
were ever invented, for whether in the hour-
glass form; the most tiresome and vulgar of
any; or in the form of a straight line hung
on a tape that always gives way at a critical
moment, or else "sags" down in the middle;
and in that of a couple of ridiculous little
curtains tied back with ribbons, they are alike
absurd and useless. White curtains, by all
means, should be used in the bedroom under
the cretonne ones, but let them be curtains,
fixed on two rods, one at the top of the
window frame, the other along the window

sill, and let the muslin be edged with frills, and stretch from the top of the window to the bottom ; and then the outside of the house will look nice, and the curtains will also be of some use, as, whether the window is opened or closed, the curtains remain fixed and stationary, and answer the purpose for which they were intended ; namely, to keep out the neighbours' eyes, and to allow of our dressing and undressing, with the window open if we are inclined to do so. The cretonne curtains lined with a dark sateen, and edged with ball-binding, draw easily over these at night, or when the sun is too bright to be comfortably borne, though sunshine should never be unreasonably shut out. The sun is the life-giver, and his rays should be courted as much as we can manage to court them, in this sunless, and fog-laden, and east wind driven country of ours.

No bedroom carpet should ever be allowed to fit the room, and as many as possible of the up-stairs carpets should be alike, as indeed should be the sets of ware. These precautions enable one, in case of a move or a series of

accidents, to mend or remake carpet No. 1 out
of carpet No. 2, or to make one good and complete set of ware out of two, when different
articles belonging to both have been smashed ;
while a square carpet fits almost any room, and
can be eked out by a wider margin of either
staining or Indian matting, or clean self-
coloured linoleum, which are the only ways of
edging carpets which should ever be allowed,
carpets fitted to the rooms ; or with felt sur-
rounds, being so many dust-traps, and serving
as so many separate dust-bins in each corner
of any room where the carpet fits exactly.

The best material of all for a bedroom floor
is, without the smallest doubt, that invaluable
material Indian matting. It is always fresh
and sweet, never allows dust to accumulate as
all carpets do, wears reasonably well, about
seven years as a rule, more with care, and
when there is but a moderate amount of traffic ;
and is invariably praised by any doctor who
has to attend a patient in a room where the
floor is covered with this healthy and capital
material. It should be about 2*s.* 8*d.* a yard,
is wide, and is to be had best from Maple and

Treloar, where can also be obtained the Kurd
rugs, which should be put about over its surface—about one large one at 28s. 6d., and two
smaller ones at 8s. 9d. each, being sufficient for
an ordinary bedroom. These can be shaken
daily if desired; they must be shaken every week
when the bedroom is thoroughly cleaned, which
in all well-regulated households is regularly
once a week. If matting cannot be afforded I
recommend a square of Wallace's "lily" carpet
in either the red, green, or blue; or else of
Pither's "cottage" carpet, or of a very useful
carpet sold by Colbourne at about 3s. the yard.
These carpets are all quite satisfactory; they
have sufficient pattern on them to avoid the
usual faults of plain carpets, but have not
enough to strike one's eye the moment one
enters the room, and in consequence no one
would soon or easily tire of them: a great
thing in their favour; as I know of carpets,
beautiful in the material if not in design or
colour; of which their owners are so heartily
tired that they would be thankful, if they
could afford to exchange the richer pile, or
Axminster, of which they are so weary for a

H

simple Kidderminster, which should have the useful non-attractive qualities, so conspicuous by their absence in their own carpets. Bed-room carpets should always be cheap ones, they can then be replaced without an undue struggle should they become dirty, and disagreeable; or be exposed to the disastrous effects of a long illness. Any one who has been ill for some time in a special room will understand what I mean; the carpet and paper and cretonne may all be well cleaned and renovated; but as long as they remain the same, the illness appears to lie in wait there; both for the patient herself and the nurses who have passed so many anxious hours there; and only complete alterations will ever obliterate the memory of that special miserable and painful time.

No other material but cretonne should be allowed in a bedroom for hangings. This is so cheap, and furthermore, can always be washed and cleaned, and if reasonable care is bestowed upon it, it would last at least ten years. I have had some of Burnett's terra-cotta rosebud cretonne up for seven years,

and it is as good as the day it was bought,
and will last seven years longer yet, I think;
while of course every one knows, and most
likely possesses, specimens of the chintzes our
grandmothers were so fond of; and which
lasted not only years, but generations, and
which is often seen in old-fashioned houses
even in these present days of ours. But even
if our cretonne will not last as long as the
chintzes used, it is so clean and healthy, that
I do hope no one will use anything else in a
sleeping room, at all events, if they value
their own health, and the delights of possess-
ing a room which always feels fresh and
bright.

Toilet-covers require a good deal more care
and attention than they have received, and so
do quilts, counterpanes, and towels, to say
nothing of sheets and pillow-cases. All these
can be made very pretty at small cost if the
housewife have only the use of her fingers;
in this case the toilet-covers and quilts should
match, and should be of coarse linen or Bolton
shirting, and should be edged with Torchon
or Greek lace, and the whole surface should

be embroidered in the style called "powdering," in tiny flowers, or else in the "love-in-the-mist" pattern, or the tiny wheel pattern, which are both school of art designs, and can be had ready to work of Francis in Hanway Street, Oxford Street. The quilts are 30s., with crewels to finish, and a large corner begun.

As the toilet-covers should fit the tables exactly, they would have to be made to order; but a clever worker could of course manage these herself; and also very likely be able to originate patterns for herself for the quilts. These should cover the bed entirely, and just clear the floor at either side and at the end of the bedstead also. The sheet, which should be frilled, and have a large monogram in the centre, should fold over the top of the bedspread or quilt, and the top pillows should be placed on this sheet in frilled and monogramed cases. Of course these cases are out of the reach of the ordinary mortal, if she cannot work herself; but if she can, she will have charming bedrooms instead of the ordinary chamber, in which is expended as little time and taste, as is compatible with cleanliness and moderate aspirations after the beautiful.

The towels should also have a monogram; and not only should the washing-stand have a high tiled back, but rails at each end for towels. This makes one article of furniture the less in the room, but does away with the clumsy horse, which is always in the way, and not unseldom gets broken and out of order. White towels with a red and blue border are the nicest, and there should be never less than three on the stand; this should include a rough towel for bath purposes, which said bath should never be taken elsewhere than in the bath-room; unless under very exceptional circumstances; then a square of linoleum and a big bath blanket should be provided, unless we wish our carpets or matting to be ruined beyond redemption. But as even quite tiny houses are provided with their bath-room, we need hardly contemplate anything so unpleasant, as being obliged to allow an ordinary bath in a bedroom.

If the toilet-covers and quilts cannot be worked, the toilet-covers should be made of

either Tunis tapestry, which has a gold thread
in, and washes remarkably well, or of serge,
which also washes.   These covers should
accurately fit the tables for which they are
required, and should furthermore be edged
with a ball fringe ; these should just fall over
the edge, but not be long enough for them to be
shut in when the drawers are open.   A couple
of trays on the toilet table to hold the brushes,
covered with small mats to match the toilet
tables, should not be forgotten ; and a box
pincushion made out of an old cigar-box, and
covered with tapestry, is an excellent addition
to the table : it serves as a *"vide-poche,"* and
also holds odds and ends generally.

The quilt should be first *always*—the ordinary honeycomb one with heavy cotton fringe ;
this is of course left on at night, but if a
worked quilt cannot be forthcoming, a large
bed-spread of cretonne should be thrown entirely over the bed during the daytime ; this
should be edged all round with a nine-inch
flounce, and should almost touch the floor in
the same way that the embroidered coverlet
would were it used.   If eider-downs are used,

they should always be in loose cretonne covers ;
these can be removed for washing, and should
be edged with a three-inch frill; these cases
should button and unbutton, and be put on
the eider-down just like an enormous pillow-
case would be.

If two people have to use one bedroom
without a dressing-room to supplement it;
and this should never be the case if it can in
any way be avoided; it is necessary that a
screen of some kind should be provided; and
as screens are so extremely cheap now-a-days
any one can compass this much-to-be-desired
addition to the furniture.   Charming screens
of all kinds can be had from Gregory in
Regent Street, where I have really seen a
beauty for 14s. 6d.; but a little more should
be given, as it should be six feet high if
possible, and should have a linen back; those
which are only paper on both sides are soon
knocked through and made shabby.   I like
also a nice fluted cretonne screen in a bedroom, but these are, as a rule, rather heavy,
and are neither as artistic nor inexpensive as
the linen-backed Japanese screens sold by

Gregory, and indeed by Maple, Liberty, or any other similar establishment.

Under the same circumstances as would necessitate a screen, it is much nicer to have two small or single washing-stands; than one big one fitted for two people. These small single stands are really very inexpensive, and are much more comfortable in every way. Corner ones are very pretty, and of course take up far less room than two quite straight ones would do. Smee has a specially pretty corner wash-stand that would be admirable for such a room as I have been thinking about. I have also seen an excellent adaptation of the sofa-ottoman at Hampton's, which should be a most useful addition to any bedroom where much space is required for clothes. Instead of the usual straight box with its curved or sofa end, the box-ottoman has a well-stuffed spring seat, and an equally well-arranged back and high ends, thus making it into a really comfortable sofa, and a nice-looking piece of furniture as well. It costs rather over £7, and would hold quite an array of dresses at full length, as regards the skirts of ordinary

walking dresses; while if placed with one end
against the wall, on one side of the fire; it
would make a comfortable place to lie down
on and rest, especially if a couple of big soft
cushions were added; and these are days when
we cannot have too many cushions placed
about, in their pretty frilled covers of the
ever-fascinating and artistic Liberty silk. A
book-case with a few well-chosen books should
be in every bedroom, as should be a cupboard
bracket for bottles and odds and ends; there
should be a square boot-cupboard, the top of
which, covered with a cloth, serves as a bed-
side table; and there should also be a couple
of candlesticks, with glass shades on, to prevent the grease being spilled all over the
carpet; and likewise a match-box should be
fastened to the wall, in such a way, that it
cannot be removed by a careless housemaid;
who should furthermore be forbidden to touch
the matches contained therein, under pain of
immediate dismissal.

I do not advise my readers ever to purchase
enamelled or what is called art furniture. If
funds will not allow of their rising above deal,

which is provided grained or otherwise spoiled
and made to simulate (very badly) maple and
other woods; this furniture should be purchased from the manufacturer before the
handles are on, or the abominable graining
begun; then at home the invaluable Aspinall
should come into play; or the equally invaluable Jackson's stains, and the deal should be
either aspinalled ivory, hedge-sparrow egg
blue, or sea green—the only three colours
which really look well in a mass—or stained
a dark brown or malachite-green, according to
taste, and the room for which the furniture
is required. Brass drop-handles should be
added—these average $4\frac{3}{4}d$. each; and if there
be a long panel in the wardrobe, this should
be left unpainted; and filled in with the
ever-useful Japanese leather paper; or with
cretonne similar to that used in draping the
windows and for the bed-spread. The paper
or cretonne should be glued on with Le Page's
liquid glue, and a better "job" is made if a
light beading of wood is placed round inside
the panel; this hides all untidynesses that are
possible, and gives a distinct finish to the

appearance. But ash or walnut should be had
whenever it is possible to afford it. These
woods will never go out of fashion, as will
undoubtedly *expensive* enamelled furniture.
Aspinall is invaluable for deal and grained
woods, and for house decoration, and should
be entirely confined to these excellent uses.
The grain of really fine woods is too lovely a
thing to be lightly cast aside, and will, I feel,
always hold its own in a satisfactory way.

I must not conclude this chapter without a
special word on the subject of the decoration
of the bedroom, and must warn my readers
against employing either terra-cotta or red for
this purpose. There is an especially odious
pinky terra-cotta which builders particularly
fancy; which I trust may soon never be seen
anywhere, and any one confronted with this
paper should demand its instant extermina-
tion. Also so-called sanitary papers should
be scouted. Sanitary papers may be able to
be washed, but I see no advantage in that;
all papers, sanitary or not, must be removed
after an infectious illness; and really papers
are so cheap and so pretty now-a-days that

no one need chose an ugly, colourless paper ;
and I have never seen a sanitary paper which
was not both ; because they can wash it.
When a paper becomes dirty enough to require washing it should be removed with hot
water and another put up. The change will
be pleasant, as well as the sense of cleanliness,
which is all we should obtain by merely washing the paper down, in a way that must make
it even more disgusting, and colourless, than it
was when it was first put up. The floral papers
of the present day are so charming that I hope
they may remain in fashion for some time.
These make ideal bedrooms with cretonne
curtains, bed-spread, and dados to match—
the best specimens are to be found at Godfrey
Giles', 19 Old Cavendish Street, and at Haines',
83 Queen Victoria Street ; and the "wild
rose" paper, stone or ivory paint, and wild
rose cretonne, green lily carpet, and malachite
green stained furniture would make a charming room. If terra-cotta paper be already on
the walls provided by the landlord, these
greens will again be found useful ; and it is
well to remember that the only way to tone

down or render the room livable in under
these circumstances is to have a quantity of
green in the room. The green lily carpet and
green stained furniture will be found invaluable here, especially if we use Helbronner's
charming 604 cretonne at 1s. 8d. a yard.
The ceiling should also be papered with
Pither's sage-green berry paper, and then the
room will be artistic, at any rate, and really as
pretty as it is possible to make it.

Another very pretty and inexpensive bedroom is made by using Pither's brown blossom
paper and all brown paint; or else "quaker
blue" paint and a "blue lily" carpet, and all
dark blue and white cretonne at 1s. a yard from
Pither, all blue and white ware, and walnut or
stained brown furniture. The ware should
always in some measure correspond with the
decorations, and in the terra-cotta and green
room should be the pretty set of "tulip ware"
sold by Wallace on purpose to harmonize with
this special scheme of colouring. As a rule,
a blue bedroom is the perfection of restful
colouring, and next comes a green one. This
naturally need not be arsenical, and of course,

unless the paper is one of Pither's, it should be properly tested. As a rule, however, these arsenical greens are not artistic, and therefore are seldom seen now. For a blue bedroom Pither's blue " bay-tree" paper at 1s. 6d. would be very pretty; all cream paint, or else all blue; a yellow and white ceiling paper from Maple at 4d. a piece, and a "red lily" carpet; the red would give the required warmth; which could be repeated in a red, green, and blue " Westminster" cretonne sold by Oetzman, which washes extremely well, and would look very nice indeed in such a room. The green could be Pither's " bay-tree," " berry," or " blossom" paper, according to the size of the room; the red carpet could be repeated here, and the cretonne could be the sage-green "poppy" cretonne also sold by Oetzmann. The red berry paper could be used as a ceiling paper, but I should prefer the pink and cream paper sold by Land, 93 Cannon Street, at 1s. a piece; the pink would harmonize with the red carpet, and should be repeated in the muslin curtains, which, if not made of Kay's India muslin frilled, or of "*guipure vitrage*," should be of Colbourne's artistic muslins in the Hawthorn pattern at $4\frac{3}{4}d$. a yard. These curtains should be frilled each side, and the frills should be full, falling softly, and should be about three and a half to five inches wide, according to the size of the window, and the way in which they were arranged.

If possible the bed should be placed with one side to the wall, and not straight out into the room, as that gives double the room for dressing that one would otherwise have; and if it is possible to afford a dado one should be added, either of cretonne or matting. These dados are run straight round the wall, and secured at the bottom with light tacks (in the case of matting slight strips of wood are put in each corner of the room to keep the matting in place), and at the top with a slight wooden rail, *screwed on*, not nailed, as screws can always be removed, and the dado taken down, washed, and put up again. The dado saves the wall tremendously, and makes a bedroom look far more finished than it could without one. In the case of a floral paper, the dado should match it as nearly as possible, but should be

run round the wall, the flowers going in an
opposite direction to those on the paper; this
breaks up the wall, and gives an excellent
decorative effect.

Even in the smallest and cheapest of houses,
where the builder and landlord have done their
worst, and where there seems no place for the
bed except between the window and the door,
with the foot in the fireplace, I cannot too
often impress upon my readers, that there is
much to be done to mitigate these disagree-
ables, if only one's eyes are continually looking
about for pretty things, and one has common-
sense.   A curtain hanging down *outside* the
door may make a bed that faces that door a
secure place of refuge ; screens are more useful
too than can be said, and now cretonnes are
so very cheap, and artistic serges abound, no
one who has the smallest eye for colour—and
she who has not, would not care, or even know
if her room were ugly or charming—need have
un ugly room or an ugly house.

Of course the great enemies to this desired
end are the landlord and the speculative
builder, and those who clamour for cheapness,

and care for nothing beside; but graining disappears before Aspinall's magic touch; and what with the charming carpets, and cretonnes to be found by taking a little trouble; no one need despair; neither need they wonder if such a paper will hang well or look nice; for all the papers I mention have been really constantly tried, and are quite perfect successes. Naturally new designs arc always coming up; the. British public joining to its mania for cheapness, that of demanding in season and out of season something new; but, thanks to Pither, Haines, and one or two other people; who realize that it is possible that a thing which is charming to-day, may be equally charming next week, or even the week after; tried and good cretonnes, papers, and carpets arc always to be had of them; and those of which I speak can and will always be had; at least as long as people ask for them; and find, as they have found now for just six years, that I am reliable, and never recommend anything I have not in some measure tried and found successful—with which conceited remark I will conclude this present chapter on bedrooms, and pass on to describe bath-rooms, nurseries, and the more prosaic but equally necessary, and in some cases equally enthralling, regions of the kitchen, basement, and offices generally.

CHAPTER VI.

NURSERIES AND BATH-ROOMS.

THE nurseries in any ordinary little house are all too often conspicuous by their absence; that is to say, any small and out-of-the-way chamber is set aside for the children, who have no place to call their own, and in consequence cannot possibly be properly brought up. It is therefore most necessary in taking a house, to consider whether there are any rooms for the younger members of the household, where they can be in a measure their own masters and mistresses; and where they can play, sleep, or do their lessons; without interfering unduly with the comfort of the heads of the establishment. It is also equally necessary that these rooms should be pretty, should have as much sunlight as possible, and should be decorated in such a manner that one can obtain the maximum of effect, with the minimum of danger, of all being ruthlessly spoiled by the small fidgets; who are never happy, it seems to us, without kicking the paint, or pulling the paper in engaging shreds off the wall.

If blue is the pleasantest colour to live with, let blue be selected for both the nurseries ; where, above all, a struggle should be made to protect the base of the wall from dilapidation by stretching a real dado round it. This need not be a very ruinous process, especially if we proceed by papering the wall with Pither's blue and cream berry paper at 1s. 6d. the piece; then there should be run round the wall a cretonne sold by Oetzmann in blue and cream at 8$\frac{3}{4}d$. the yard, called the Westminster; the dado rail and all the paint should be Aspinall's hedge-sparrow egg blue; and the short full frilled curtains should also be of the Westminster cretonne, lined with a dark blue sateen, and edged with a gauffered frill. Ball fringe is too tempting for a nursery, for what small hand could resist the fascinating employment of pulling the balls off the braid, one after the other, to use as weapons of warfare, or else as pills for the dolls of the establishment? Above all, let there be no blinds in these rooms, the cretonne curtains are quite enough protection against ordinary sunshine; and thus endless expense and worry will be saved. Blinds are *generally* out of order in the down-stairs apartments; they are *always* in a state of untidiness and coming to grief, in any room where there are small children about.

The simpler the furniture is in a nursery the better. I have advocated for large rooms, where money is no object, a complete series of fitments round the chamber, in order that there may be no corners for the small heads to knock against; and if paterfamilias is clever with his fingers, I see no reason why something should not be managed on the same lines, if on a much smaller scale. If there are any recesses in the room; shelves should be fitted in, as deeply as can be managed; from the top of the room to the bottom, and a couple of cupboard doors should protect these shelves from unholy ravages. On the top shelves should be kept the best toys, on the next the nursery

tea-cups and saucers; and the bottom shelves
should be given up to the children; who can
keep their treasures on one shelf divided into
as many partitions as there are children; and
on the other side the shelves can be made into
a regular dolls' house. The front of each room
could have a tiny curtain to protect it from
the vulgar gaze and from the dust. Nothing
used to tumble over on our heads oftener than
did the dolls' house. Such a catastrophe is
obviated by locating it inside a cupboard;
which, being flush with the mantelpiece jambs;
would have no corners, and would be in an
unbroken line from wall to wall.

No food of any sort or kind should be kept
in the nurseries, and this rule should be en-
forced strictly by the mistress. Nurses are
unaccountably fond of hoarding, and bits of
stale bread, cake, ends of butter, and driblets
of milk; are often put away and forgotten in a
cupboard kept entirely for the nursery things.
If the cupboard is shared with the children
the doors are more or less always open, and
hoarding becomes impossible; the only bit of
hoarding that should be allowed being morsels

of old linen and venerable pocket-handker-
chiefs, invaluable for dressing wounds, and when
colds are in the ascendant ; "pieces" may also
be kept for patching knees and elbows, and
for making patchwork of ; and, in fact, a piece
bag should be in every nursery, for are there
not always impecunious dolls to be looked
after, and kept decently supplied with garments of all sorts and sizes ?   There should,
if in any way possible ; be a window-seat, wide
and strong, to stand jumping upon.   I should
advise a wide wooden shelf on four or six
stout legs like a long thin table ; the proper
height from the ground, generally about
sixteen inches.   This should be very wide,
and should have some cushions covered in
Liberty's arras cloth, which looks as if it were
warranted to stand any amount of knocking
about.   These cushions should be tied tightly
over the shelf or seat, and should be supplemented by a soft shawl and a couple of pillows ;
should a small invalid require a place to lie
down and rest ; albeit in every nursery there
should be some kind of a sofa available for
these occasions, which occur unfailingly in

every house where there are any children at all.
A very good addition to the window-seat is a
species of barricade on the principle of the
sides of a crib ; this can be secured with hooks
to eyes fastened in the wall, and should be at
the two ends and along the front ; this allows
small children of two and three, to play un-
molested and out of harm's way ; and to look
out of the window without being in the way
of their elders. They can amuse themselves
in this manner for hours, and are absolutely
out of danger, either to themselves or from
others ; and a similar platform saves a nurse
the fatigue of holding up a heavy child to
gaze out at the passing vehicles—a never-
failing entertainment if the nursery window
overlooks a busy street.

With the exception of the cupboard, a high
fender fixed to the wall, a round table, the
top of which should be covered with oil cloth
strongly sewn on, and some chairs ; no regular
furniture would be required. The chairs should
be strong enough to stand a good deal of knocking about, and the ordinary Windsor or kitchen
chair is as good a thing as possible ; but there

should of course be high chairs, and a comfortable seat for the nurse : this should be low and wide, and she should moreover have a big work-basket standing on a smaller table which she could move with her chair and the inevitable baby out of reach when the fun is becoming fast and furious. The deep wicker chair cushioned in arras cloth, and unpainted, that Colbourne sells, is a capital seat for nurse, that should be forbidden to the children, otherwise it would soon be utterly spoiled and done for.

The question of floor covering is a very vexed one. Some authorities recommend linoleum it is so clean and sweet; but I do not agree with them; it is clean, undoubtedly, but it is dreadfully cold to the feet, and very uncomfortable for a crawling child ; and I should be inclined to state positively, that nothing is better than stained edges to the boards, and a fringed square of Brussels carpet fastened down with carpet pins. A small child if put down to crawl, can be provided with a crawling rug; which, if properly embellished with impossible animals, in Turkey red cloth, stitched to a warm water-proofed blanket, keeps it amused and within bounds, and nothing else need hurt the carpet. Brussels is very long-suffering, and bears an amount of traffic, and even ill-usage that nothing else will. If people are not particularly anxious to be artistic: (and this is a thing that should never be allowed, especially in a nursery, where the eye is trained insensibly more than people think); very good Brussels carpet can be bought in ugly colourings at Maple's, who sells these carpets off cheaply; either because the colourings have been proved a failure, or because the fickle public demands something new at their hands. I should advise a good red carpet in this room; Wallace's " Stella " in Brussels at 3s. 11d. a yard would do excellently, and would wear quite as long as it is healthy for a carpet to last anywhere.

The night nursery could be papered and painted in the same way as that suggested for the day nursery; but even if baths are obliged to be had in the room; and when they are very small the children must be bathed in the room in which they sleep; I should advise the floor being covered with

the despised linoleum,—in a self colour; dark
brown is the best shade; and by each bed, in
front of the toilet table and washing-stand, I
should put down one of the striped blue and
white dhurries sold by Maple or Liberty for
about 2s. each; these wash splendidly, and
last for years. A large art blanket should be
put down by the side of the bath, for the child
to step out upon; and two of these useful
articles should be in use. I do not forget
even now the damp, abominable feel of a bath
blanket on which my predecessors had been
placed while nurse dried them. A dry blanket
should be provided for each child—No. 1 being
dried while No. 2 was in use, and so on. These
blankets are to be had inexpensively in artistic
colourings from Mansergh and Son, Lancaster;
they should be edged by coarse crewel button-
hole stitches; and are greatly improved by a
big monogram in the corner; or one of Brigg's
devices ironed off and worked over with the
same kind of crewels; but the button-holing
will be quite sufficient for a nursery, and the
grander decoration can be saved for the bath-
room proper, where the bigger children should

be encouraged to wash themselves; as soon as they can be trusted in that fascinating spot.

The furniture in a night nursery should consist of a plain double washing-stand in ash, with only one set of ware thereon; with a plain toilet table in ash with drawers down each side, and a good glass; of a chest of drawers, and as large a wardrobe as can be managed. Even in a large room the nurse should never have more than two children with her, or two and a baby at the most; and the beds should be as far apart as possible, uncurtained, and without valances to act as dust traps, and to encourage untidy habits. The nurse's bed and the childrens' should have Excelsior mattresses and one hair mattress each; only one pillow and a bolster; and no accumulations and puttings away should be allowed in a sleeping room. Clothes that are stored from one season to another should be stored elsewhere; there should be nothing of the kind allowed where there are any children.

If a change of decoration is desired, a very pretty and suitable one, and one that would not clash, with that in the day nursery; if the

two rooms opened into each other, as they
ought to do, would be to paper the wall with
Pither's brown blossom paper, adding a dado
of Pither's dark blue and white cretonne
at 1s. the yard; the paint should be dark
blue also, the ceiling colour-washed cream;
and the curtains of Pither's dark blue and
white cretonne lined with dark blue; yellow
and white muslin could be placed on the
window here, as the children would not care
to look out from this special room, where they
should never be allowed, once they are up and
dressed; and where the beds and room itself
should be most thoroughly ventilated. Even
in wet weather the windows should be open
for at least an hour and a half, and the beds
put in a thorough draught between the window
and the door; and on fine days all the blankets
and counterpanes should be shaken daily out
of doors, the beds being put to air in the
sunshine; which should be allowed to pour
unchecked into the room; which should, if
possible, be so placed that it would receive all
the morning sun; the afternoon sun making
the rooms very hot for the children to sleep

in. If the afternoon sun comes into the night nursery, the room must be protected from the heat by some kind of sun-blind; and great comfort is also given in an ordinary slated house; where the nurseries are on the top floor, by having the roof whitewashed about May. This adds considerably to the coolness and comfort of top rooms, and should never be neglected if possible, a hot bedroom being of all things the most unhealthy and disagreeable.

Whatever hints I may give about a nursery, all would be incomplete without some words about the pictures which are hung up for the children to look at. There are few households where a grandpapa or grandmama, godmother or aunt does not exist; who gives the children occasionally expensive toys; these are, as a rule, too grand to be played with, and are put away for special occasions, which not unseldom never come. I remember quite a regiment of these toys which went to a hospital at our first clearing out, preparatory to a move. Now how much more sensible it would be if grandmama bought one of the fascinating dog pictures of which we see so

many specimens now-a-days, and hung it up
in the nursery; it could of course belong to
any individual child—in that case the child's
name should be written on the back in grandmama's own writing; but it would be a joy to
them all, and give pleasure and teach lessons
no smart ladylike doll or "uneasy" mechanical
toy ever could—"uneasy" being nursery talk
for anything that is not mastered in a moment;
or that requires great care in the manipulation.
Children notice much more than people realize;
they absorb nice or disagreeable habits marvel-
lously, and become in a great measure what
they are formed by their first impressions;
and they will never care for good and pretty
things, unless they are in some measure
familiarized with them from their earliest days;
which is another reason why the nursery
should be prettily furnished and papered, and
why the children should be taught to appre-
ciate, and properly care for their own particular
room.

In the perfect house for which we all
long, and which the wiles of the speculative
builder prevent us from enjoying, there will

undoubtedly be no doors jutting out into the room, but all will slide comfortably and quietly into a groove in the wall; but if this is impossible, great care should be taken to protect the door in some way from injuring the small people, who are too apt to run against it and knock their heads. I should advise the door being made to open into the passage, and in front of the opening a small gate should be put inside the nursery, in a similar style, to the gates placed at the head of the stairs, to prevent the children falling down them. This allows of the door being left open for ventilation, and prevents the smaller children going into the passage; while if the door opens into the passage itself the children cannot knock their heads, as they so often do, cutting them open in a ghastly manner.

That reminds me that every nursery should have its simple medicine chest, provided with camphor for colds, arnica for strains, calendula for cuts, and sweet oil for stings and burns; and furthermore, simple rules should be written out and printed, and hung on the walls, telling a nurse what to do in an emergency, and until the doctor comes. These simple rules can be, I think, had from the National Health Society for a few pence, but if not the family doctor would soon do this for one. Yet nothing will save a child so much suffering as early lessons of obedience! Once make a child obedient, and it is saved many a hard blow, mental and physical. But my space is too limited to allow of my dwelling on this side of the picture, and I will therefore pass away from ethics to shortly regard the bath-room, which should not be placed too far away from the rooms given to the children. If it is, endless colds are caught going thither and returning; and in this case baths must be taken in the children's rooms.

The bath-room should be papered with a pretty tiled patterned paper, which should be sized and varnished; this prevents the steam from spoiling the paper as speedily as it otherwise would. The paint should be Aspinall's ivory, for a bath-room cannot look too clean and fresh; and the floor should be covered with linoleum, on which should be laid one of the bath blankets of which I spoke before.

K

Of course a perfect bath-room should be tiled, there is no doubt of that, and the edge of the bath should also be tiled; nothing spoils so quickly as the wooden edge of the bath; for nothing will cure people; children especially; from depositing the soap anywhere on the polished border. But as tiles are out of the question, the edge of the bath should either be carefully covered with American leather, or else painted with Aspinall's bath enamel. That resists hot water, and remains tidy some time, and can always be renewed at any moment; as can the enamelling on the iron bath itself, without the expense and annoyance of sending it away to be re-stoved; but if an amateur attempts to paint the bath, particular attention must be given to the directions on the tin containing the enamel, and above all the bath; when it is painted and presumably dry; should be filled with cold water, which must stand for twenty-four or better still for forty-eight hours in the bath. This hardens the enamel thoroughly, and allows it to stand successfully the very hottest water possible.

The bath-room should be furnished very,

very simply, and should have little in it beside
a chair for the garments of the bather, a
basket fastened on the wall to hold the sponges,
and a large floating bowl to hold the soap; it
should have a fixed towel rail at the side of
the bath, and the maid must be obliged to see
that the towels thereon are thoroughly dried.
Only two large bath sheets should be kept in
the bath-room, as most people carry their own
towels in with them. Above the bath should
be three shelves enamelled with the bath
enamel, and here the different hot water cans
of the household should be kept. Each room
should have its own can, and great care should
be taken that these cans are kept for the
special rooms. The enamelled art cans sold
by Whiteley for about 3s. 9d. each are very
nice; the best, however, are the plain brass
cans—these require great care to keep them
bright, and cost about 7s. 9d. or 8s. each, also
at Whiteley's.

No place should be kept more scrupulously
clean than should a bath-room, and the servant
who dares to wash bedroom ware; or even
empty her pail down a bath; (and this I have

actually known a maid to do), should be
punished with a month's warning on the spot;
and indeed she should be dismissed at once,
if the month's wages and board wages can be
afforded, as she must be hopelessly dirty to do
anything so very disagreeable; and I advise
not only an inspection of all the drains of a
house before a house is taken, but that special
inspection be given to the bath and its outlet;
more than one illness of which I have heard
being clearly traceable to the fact, that in some
mysterious manner, some gas came up through
the place where the water ran away; and
poisoned the entire household more or less.
If the window is large, and the room is in
consequence overlooked, I should advise the
glass being entirely covered by Graham and
Biddle's excellent imitation of cathedral glass.
This is put on squares of glass, and these in
their turn are placed on the existing glass,
fastened in at the four corners with nails;
thus the material is between two pieces of
glass, and is not exposed either to the weather
or the effects of the steam. Muslin and
cretonne soon become untidy and damp in a

bath-room, but this would obscure the glass; which could furthermore be rendered opaque, by hanging a reed blind straight down over it; but if regular curtains are required muslin could be stretched right over the window as suggested before, with the serge curtains to draw at night. A bell should be in every bath-room, where also should be some means of ventilation, and it would be a wise thing were the door never to be locked, a placard with "occupied," or "in use" written on hanging outside the door, to denote that it was in use. So many people have fainted and actually died in a hot bath; who could have been saved had the room been accessible; that I think these precautions should be taken in the case of any one who was suspected of heart disease, or of being subject to fits; or a double latch could be made, which could be opened from outside in an emergency, and would give more sense of security than would be obtained from the hanging out of the placard.

CHAPTER VII.

THE KITCHENS, BASEMENT, AND SERVANTS' ROOMS.

THE kitchen is generally the last place in the house that is given over to the artistic decorator; but those who saw the complete and charming artisan's kitchen at the Manchester Exhibition, designed and executed by Mr. Armitage of Stamford House, Altrincham, must have been struck with the fact, that much could be done for this despised portion of the home; were only a tithe of the money, spent uncomplainingly on almost every other corner of the fabric, devoted to its embellishment; of course in a reasonable way. Many people still consider that white-washed ceilings, "coloured" walls, and grained paint are the only proper ways of managing this place; but as picture are naturally regularly out of place here, I do plead for something a little more artistic than the smeared dun-coloured wall and drab paint; which are all, far too many servants have to contemplate from one week's end to the other. In my present house the kitchens were painted drab, and colour washed a paler shade of this same delectable hue; but great changes for the better were made by using a tiled varnished paper from Haines at 2s. the piece, an Arabian brown paint,—not enamel, but ordinary house paint,—and by a new coat of whitewash on the ceiling. No one would have known the place again, particularly after short full cretonne curtains in dark blue were added—this particular dark gray blue and white cretonne of Liberty's at 1s. the yard boiling and washing "like a rag," as the servants themselves say. The tiled paper can be wiped over daily with a damp duster if necessary to remove any greasy finger-marks; while the paint, having its last coat mixed with varnish, can be treated in the same way, and wiped over when it appears the worse for smoke at all. Of course the floor must be covered with a good linoleum;

the boards in a usual builder's house do not
allow of the scrubbed spotless floors which
were our great-grandmother's pride; but if
the cook is careful; she should be given a
rug, or good square of carpet lined with thin
American leather, to put down when her work
is done; and she should also have a tablecloth
which can be easily washed; a good serge is as
good as anything; to make the kitchen nice on
Sunday afternoon, or when the maids have a
friend to tea; here all is easily cleaned; yet
all is immeasurably superior to the ordinary
washed kitchen.

I have found a regular dado of oil-cloth a
wonderful protection, both to the walls of a
kitchen where there was much unavoidable
wear and tear; and to the base of the wall
leading up the back stairs; and this is a thing
to be remembered where really hard wear is
unavoidable, as it undoubtedly is in a narrow
passage; where boxes are carried up and down,
and where trays are carried past; and where
tradesmen's messengers lounge about waiting
for orders; with their backs against the wall;
and their ready fingers, in the case of small

errand boys ; engaged in digging holes in the
plaster, and tearing off bits of paper, or of the
usual colour wash. But I have yet to find
the material which will successfully withstand
the wear and tear of the kitchen stairs, and at
present have to content myself with Treloar's
crimson cocoa-nut matting. On ordinary stair-
cases this wears splendidly ; it does fade, there
is no denying that, but it does not go into rags
for a couple of years, or even three. True it
does not last longer on the especial stairs of
which I am thinking ; still as the ordinary Dutch
carpet cuts out into strips in six months, these
stairs must be particularly trying specimens, I
fancy. This particular make of cocoa-nut matting can be had in brown, in crimson, and also
in dark green, and answers very well for passages in the basement, where one must have
some covering down, or else the noise of the
perpetual footsteps to and fro would drive one
wild.

The ordinary table in the window for sew-
ing, and the servants' meals, should be distinct
and separate from that on which much of the
work is done. Every house, even quite small

houses, ought to have a room in which the servants could sit; yet that has never yet been accomplished except in big houses, really more like mansions than anything else; but until the perfect house is built, the kitchen should be made as comfortable as may be. But the ordinary wooden chair must be still *de rigueur*, for, uncomfortable as they are, they are the only chairs that resist the steam and mess of the kitchen, and the rather severe usage they receive at the servants' hands. There should be a chair each for the maids, and two for their visitors, not more; and if an old stout sofa can be bought at a sale, and covered either with American leather or horse-hair, it might be placed here, not as inducement to be idle, but as a resting place after work, which surely must result in causing a longing for a less hard and unbending seat, or lounge, than that afforded by the Windsor chair.

It is an excellent thing to encourage a cat in a kitchen; it makes the place home-like a once, and furthermore keeps down the mice. A large cupboard for stores which require to be kept dry is a good addition to the kitchen;

but candles and currants must not be kept there—candles bend in the most peculiar way, and currants dry up until they are like chips. Almost anything else can be retained in a kitchen cupboard, but these two articles really must not.

The basement should be kept particularly sweet and clean, and should be scrubbed out once a week, and whitewashed once a year, and painted once in five years; the paper, more especially if it be protected at the base by the oil-cloth dado, will last years, and indeed, as far as the dado itself is concerned, practically for ever. This looks far more cheerful than any other arrangement, and the tiled varnished papers are generally pretty enough to please even a most fastidious eye; though a perfectly ideal basement I once saw was walled with tiles themselves, and rather spoiled one for any less costly notion.

There is very often, especially in small houses, a room in the basement that is meant, and not unseldom has to be used, for a dining-room; if this be case, the room cannot be furnished too simply, as it cannot be healthy

to sit there. It generally has none of the few
advantages possessed by the kitchen; and has
a damp, underground odour pervading it, that
no amount of fires seems able to successfully
combat; therefore it should be kept simply
for meals, and never entered unless one is
positively obliged to do so. These basement
rooms are a great drawback to many small
houses, and a basement kitchen, even in a
large house, is always to be deprecated; it
causes an extra servant's work, and the smell
of dinner never seems to leave a house where
the kitchen is underneath the other rooms.

If the kitchen is on the same floor as the sitting-rooms, there should be either a swing door
covered with baize, and covered with a curtain
on one of Maple's rods; or else a couple of curtains between the kitchen and the hall; this
deadens the sound most successfully, and keeps
out the odours. The curtain on the kitchen door
itself should be of two or even three thicknesses
of Bolton sheeting; this washes for ever, and is
a very stout material. The curtain in the hall
should of course harmonize with the hall itself;
and should only be looped back when the

maids carry in and out the things for the different meals. But often there is a "hatch" in modern houses into the kitchen itself, which would obviate any carrying in and out of the room; in this case a curtain of American leather should be hung down inside the hatch; this would prevent any one who was seated opposite the hatch seeing straight into the kitchen; and being of American leather it could be sponged should it become greasy, or touch the meat or vegetables. Another excellent idea is to have a shaped shelf just below the hatch; a straight one looks a little too formal; this should be painted to match the rest of the paint, and should have a fine linen cloth laid along it; and here could be arranged spare spoons and forks, and finger-glasses, odds and ends generally; while above the hatch is placed another narrow shelf made from Giles' bracket rail: this finishes it off, and gives another receptacle for odds and ends of china. This looks well, and gives the hatch a far more ornamental appearance than it could possibly have without something of the kind. The hatch saves a great deal of traffic, and should be placed in any new house where the kitchen is in its proper place, namely, just behind the dining-room.

The servants' bedrooms demand just a few words before the end of this pamphlet, for nowhere is the careful mistress so "non-plussed"—if one can use such an expression—as in these chambers. Do what one may, they are never tidy, and are in a state of chaos from one "spring clean" to another. The regular dismal old-fashioned graining would be useful in these rooms, as no sort of banging about appears to harm that hideous paint, and this is no doubt the reason it has remained in favour for so long; and it would be well to have doors and wainscoting grained here, to have the dado of oilcloth and rail advised for the kitchen—the rail to be also grained, and a good sanitary paper on the walls; these papers could be washed down once a year, and the ceiling whitewashed. The furniture should be as simple as possible, and should consist of a bed for each servant. Smee, 89 Finsbury Pavement, has some admirable and inexpensive beds suitable for servants and young people generally; there is an arrangement of laths which simulate springs, and over this there is a good mattress of hair. Nothing can be simpler or more comfortable; and once a year these beds should be throughly inspected, as should, in fact, every single thing appertaining to a servant's room; they cannot help hoarding, and they will smash, and would rather go on with any amount of discomfort, than confess they had broken or damaged the property committed to their care.

Each servant should have her chest of drawers, and her own washing-stand, with a brass or iron rail for the towels, which should be at the rate of two each; the toilet-glass should be hung on the wall, or placed on the chest of drawers, which serves also as a toilet table; this should have a clean blue and white cloth, changeable twice a month. Each servant should have two coloured blankets, and a heavy blue and white counterpane, and should have three or even four in winter should she desire to have more. Of course each bed is provided with an under-blanket; this can be either an ordinary coloured blanket, or an old

one retired from service.   The furniture itself
should be grained and varnished, and should
be had from Wallace, who provides ample
plenishing for a single servant's room for
£4 ; this moreover includes the bed.   The floor
should be left bare, and by each bed and
washing-stand should be put down a dhurry ;
these wash splendidly, and are pretty and
warm.   Old carpets, or anything which har-
bours dust, should never be allowed for one
moment in these rooms ; and if there should
be a box-room, the servants should be re-
quested to keep their boxes there.   Nothing
spoils a room like keeping a box in it ; no
one seems able to resist opening and closing
it in such a way that a morsel of paper comes
off at each movement, or else a hole is dug in
the wall, and all is desolation !

It may appear absurd to dwell so continuously on keeping a house nicely, as well as
making it pretty by careful decoration and
furniture properly chosen and arranged ; but
it is absurd to decorate and furnish artistically
if the owner of the house does not intend to
keep it in order afterwards.   I have con-

stantly been both pained and annoyed by
seeing houses I have carefully decorated and
superintended, and which I have left in perfect
order, in about a couple of years made so dirty
and untidy that all the work has to be done
over again, solely, so it seems to me, to be spoiled
once more.   It is far better, if people will not
tend their homes, that they should be content
with marble halls and grained paint; these
things require no attention, and simply serve
to cover the walls of the place we dwell in.   A
house treated like that can never be in any
sense of the word a home.   These are days of
hurry, I know; everything must be had and
done at once; folks have "no time," and in
consequence year after year the reforms we
so anxiously advocate only advance slowly
indeed.   There is absolutely no necessity in
these days for the poorest person in the land
to be surrounded by ugly things; for cheap
things are quite as beautiful, and indeed sometimes even more beautiful; than the dear things
so eagerly placed under our notice by the shopman who has things to sell; who all too often
has not a particle of taste, and who is anxious

L

alone to get rid of his property ; to fill a house, not to furnish a house in the way it should be furnished, with simple plain things, and above all with colours which in this dull climate of ours, have an immense if unknown influence on us ; and which can make our houses cheerful or dull, according as we arrange them.

I do believe in colour—in real bright, glowing colour ! Nothing gives one so much joy as the sight of admirably arranged colours ; and though I was told by an eminent if rather sad decorator the other day that decorations were becoming "far too noisy," I do not care ; if the noise is the powerful blare of the trumpet of scarlet, the delicious bright warble of yellow, and the soft song of blue, or pink, or cream, by all means let us have the noise ! I maintain our skies, and, alas ! far too many of our lives, are sad enough without our making them still more doleful between sage-green walls, or in rooms decorated in dull, dead colours, that resemble nothing so much as bad pea-soup, or the fogs which hang about our chimneys, and pounce upon us when we issue from our front doors. Let therefore the would-be maker of a home sit down carefully before he undertakes the work, and if he has no taste, let him have the courage to say so. He may live in the wilds of the country ; he may not have at his fingers' ends the newest papers and the best arrangements to make ; and let him get some one whose taste has been proved to help him about the place ; let him state boldly his ideas on the subject, for after all he has to live in the house, and not his adviser ; and his tastes should of course be consulted entirely ; but if they are inadmissable, he can soon be shown why they should be altered, and ten chances to one he will see the reason ; and will acknowledge that there are more things on earth in the way of artistic furnishing than he had dreamed of in his philosophy ; and that his home can be made a real home, a real pleasure, at one half the cost ; if he will be advised by any one who knows exactly what is in the market, where it is to be had ; and has no possible interest in advising one firm more than another ; the sole anxiety being to obtain what is required, no matter from where it comes, so long as it is pretty and inexpensive.

If people too are afraid of themselves and
of charming combinations of colour, they can
always remember two or three small things on
which I have dwelt at greater length in the
chapters on the different rooms, viz. that blue
is the colour of all colours for a morning-room,
or even in which one spends much daylight
time; that red is an admirable dining-room
colour; and that yellow and white make a
capital drawing-room; not gold and white, the
dreadful white paper with gold stars which
used to be the thing not so very long ago;
but a clear, delightful, buttercup yellow and
creamy white to be found in Pither's "special
berry" papers, and of course elsewhere too.
They can also remember that Pither's papers,
Smee, Haines, and Giles are absolutely safe;
and that paint should never be picked out in
any way, but should be an even surface of
one colour; that a linen or paper dado and
imitation paper rail should never be allowed;
that a dado should be exactly a yard from the
top of the wainscot; and a frieze never less
than twelve inches, eighteen is better, and in
some rooms a frieze to the top of the door is

best of all; that all pictures should hang from
a frieze rail; and that if they require daring
combinations of colour, they should be tried
first in very cheap materials and on a small
scale, for fear they should not be as successful
as was imagined.

Curtains should be short, full, and never
looped in any manner; blinds should never be
allowed, neither should heavy cornices and
draperies be permitted; all carpets should be
square; none should fit the rooms; and finally,
above all, that the house must be constantly
looked after, and kept year by year in repair.
There is always something to be done in a
house, there is no doubt about that; and
unless that something is done at the time, we
wake up to find we have all to do together in
an expensive style; which is vexatious, beside
being often excessively inconvenient.

It is bad policy to let a house get into a state
of disrepair. Small things are not felt, but it
is vexatious to have to do all at once. A coat
of paint given occasionally,—and in these
days of aspinall one can give that oneself if
one has ordinary common-sense,—a new ceiling

paper, or wall paper above the dado, which lasts one's lifetime if properly managed, are things which cost little in themselves, but which mount up prodigiously when the house is vacated, and we have to set to work to put it in order for an incoming tenant; or even when the dirt becomes too great to be borne, and we have to do it for ourselves; it is therefore much better to keep things in good order. Once let them get beyond us, and the expense of putting all to rights is absolutely ruinous, for neglected paint often means rotten wood-work; and dirty paper and ceilings encourage small animals, which eat away the wall itself, and make structural repairs as necessary as decorative ones. It is therefore very short-sighted policy to allow one's house to get into a state of decay; for this costs far more than a certain annual expenditure on paint and paper possibly could. Of course the British workman is the great bar in the way of paint and paper; not only do the worst specimens of their kind seem told off for house decoration—specimens who drink at the smallest or indeed at *no* provocation at all,

and cannot tell black from white in consequence of these vagaries,—but the very slowest
in the world ; and one often feels inclined to
snatch the brush out of the lazy hand, and
apply it oneself. But it is always possible to
find a couple of handy men who will work
under one's own directions, and who will be
sober and tolerably quick, if they undertake
the work by contract, and are bound over to
execute it within a certain space of time. If
men are put in by a local decorator, and given
carte blanche, they take up their residence in
a house, and never leave it unless they are
absolutely turned out by their enraged victim.
A couple of men can paint and paper a room,
or a hall and passage comfortably, or do up
the kitchens, etc., which is another reason for
doing things by degrees, and a little each
separate year.

Above all, let nothing be done in a hurry ;
do not allow yourselves to be talked into
accepting an ugly paper by the landlord, or
by any one else. Before you set out to furnish
or decorate, choose your papers, at home if
you can, from the books all good firms are

always wishing to send out; and having decorated your house, furnish it as simply as possible until you have begun to live in it; then you will soon discover what other articles of furniture it requires, and will be able to complete your work in a leisurely manner. Indeed the best hint of all that can be given to those about to furnish is the sentence I have put on my title-page, " *Festina Lente* "— make haste slowly. Were this always the motto of the would-be maker of a home, there would be far more lovely and artistic homes in the world, aye, even among those we are pleased to call the lower classes, than there are at present.

THE END.

R. Clay & Sons, Limited, London & Bungay.

SMEE and COBAY,

Furniture Manufacturers & Decorators,

89 FINSBURY PAVEMENT, LONDON

(Close to Moorgate Street Railway Station).

DESIGNS, PLANS, AND ESTIMATES

SUBMITTED FREE OF CHARGE FOR

Interior Decorating

AND

FURNISHING OF HOUSES, HOTELS, and CLUBS.

WORKS:
KING HENRY'S WALK,
Ball's Pond Road, London.

M

STRODE & CO.,

GAS & ELECTRIC LIGHT ENGINEERS.

𝕬𝕣𝕥 𝕸𝕖𝕥𝕬𝕝 𝖂𝖔𝖗𝖐𝖊𝖗𝖘.

Nᵒ 5611.
£ 3.3.0.

Shade
extra

BRASS, COPPER
AND
WROUGHT IRON
Floor Lamps,
Table Lamps,
Electroliers.

CHANDELIERS,
BRACKETS,
SCONCES,
GATES,
GRILLES,
FENDERS.

Works and Show Rooms:
48 Osnaburgh St., N.W.,
Nr. Portland Rd. Station.

Branch Show Rooms:
188 Piccadilly, W.;
67 St. Paul's Ch. Yd., E.C.,
LONDON.

WM. WALLACE & CO.,

ART FURNITURE MANUFACTURERS,

151, 152, 153, CURTAIN ROAD, LONDON, E.C.

Established 1845.

Wm. WALLACE & Co.'s New Book of Registered Designs of Inexpensive Art Furniture, 9th Edition, sent post free on application. *Just Published.*

Wm. WALLACE & Co. invite all about to furnish to inspect their extensive stock of Bedroom, Dining-room, and Drawing-room Furniture; special care being given to obtain the most Artistic Designs at the lowest possible cost. Soundness of construction guaranteed. **All Goods carriage paid to any station in the United Kingdom.**

Just Published. A special Catalogue of New Artistic Furniture specially designed for and approved by Mrs. Panton. Sent post free on application on receipt of private card.

Wm. WALLACE & Co., 151, 152, 153, CURTAIN ROAD, E.C.

Established 1845.

Wholesale Furniture Manufacturers & Complete House Furnishers.

"BORDERED"

TABLE-COVERS

AND BEDSPREADS

Made to order in four days in any combinations of colour or material selected. From 1 yard to 2½ yards wide, any length.

PRICE LIST AND PATTERNS ON APPLICATION.

B. BURNET & Co., ART DRAPERS,

41 & 42, King Street, Covent Garden, London.

LANCASTER WINDOW BLINDS.

The cheapest and best in New Patterns and Colourings.
Pattern Books post free.

LANCASTER BLANKETS AND FLANNELS.

The best procurable, in White, Scarlet, and Natural.
Pattern Books post free.

LANCASTER LINOLEUM.

The cheapest in the world. Any length cut, from **1s.** square yard.
Pattern Books post free.

LANCASTER ART BLANKETS.

For Sofa Blankets, Portières, Bath Rugs, &c., in Sky, Coral, Navy, Old Gold,
Cardinal, Bronze, Peacock, Terra Cotta, &c.
33in. by 36in., **3s. 6d.** pair; 50 in. by 68 in., **7s. 6d.** pair; 54 in. by 76 in. **9s. 6d.**
pair; 60 in. by 91 in., **11s. 6d.** pair. *Pattern Books post free.*

LANCASTER ART SERGES.

In all Art Shades, 54in. wide, **2s.** yard. Plushettes, all colours, 50in. wide,
2s. 11d. yard. *Pattern Books post free.*

LANCASTER CALICOES & SHEETINGS, wear well.

Unequalled for durability. *Pattern Books post free.*

Box of Patterns of House Furnishing Novelties free on application.

ANY LENGTH CUT. CARRIAGE PAID.

MANSERGH & SON, LANCASTER.

ESSEX & Co.'s WESTMINSTER
WALL PAPERS.

TRADE MARK.

The various Wall Papers referred to in this work by Mrs. PANTON can be seen with
very many others at our **SHOW ROOMS AND LONDON OFFICES,
116 VICTORIA STREET, WESTMINSTER**—from whence also Patterns can be had.

COOKERY BOOKS Published by S. LOW & Co.

THE SKILFUL COOK. By Mary Harrison. Crown 8vo,
cloth, 5s.

ROYAL COOKERY BOOK. By Jules Gouffé. Domestic
and High-class Cookery. Household Edition. Crown 8vo, cloth, 10s. 6d.

366 MENUS AND 1,200 RECIPES OF THE BARON BRISSE.
By MRS. MATTHEW CLARK. Crown 8vo, boards, leather back, 5s.

Any of the above sent post free on receipt of price by the Publishers.

SAMPSON LOW, MARSTON, SEARLE & RIVINGTON, Limited,
St. Dunstan's House, Fetter Lane, London.

INCOME TAX : How to get it Refunded. Practical Instructions for Assessment and Appeal. With full directions for obtaining from the Inland Revenue Repayment of Tax deducted &c., whenever the Income is under £400. Also Repayment of Tax from Pay, Pension, Annuities, Coupons, Dividends, Rent, Interest, on over-assessed Professional, Trade, and Farming Profits, and on Life Insurance Premiums, &c. By ALFRED CHAPMAN, Esq. Sixth Revised Edition. Cloth, price 1s.; post free, 13 stamps.

There is scarcely a person who cannot get his Assessment reduced, and overpaid or wrongly deducted Income Tax refunded, by following these clear instructions.

See also "The Art of Housekeeping," by Mrs. HAWEIS, p. 19.

Uniform with the above, by the same Author.

INHABITED HOUSE DUTY : How and when to Appeal. Practical Instructions for Valuation and Assessment. With full directions as to Exemptions and Allowances, and how to claim them.

No Owner or Occupier of a House or Tenement should be without this most useful Book.

HOW TO APPEAL AGAINST YOUR RATES. With Forms and Full Instructions. By ANDREW DOUGLAS LAWRIE, Esq., M.A., of the South Eastern Circuit, Barrister-at-Law. Cloth, price 1s.; post free, 13 stamps.

This Book gives Owners and Occupiers of Property a clear notion of how and when to appeal against their Rates, if they are over-assessed.

HOUSE-OWNERS, HOUSEHOLDERS, AND LODGERS : Their Rights and Liabilities, also their Rights as Voters. By JOSCELYN AUGUSTUS DE MORGAN, Esq., B.A., of Lincoln's Inn, Barrister-at-Law. Cloth, price 1s. 6d.; post free, 20 stamps.

This Comprehensive Guide contains Practical Instructions as to taking, occupying, and giving up a House, with Appendix of Forms, Notices, &c.

INCOME TAX GRIEVANCES AND THEIR REMEDY. By ALFRED CHAPMAN, Esq. Post free, 3½d.

The late Lord Addington in acknowledging the receipt of a copy of the Pamphlet, wrote to the Author: "I have read your work with much approval, and it will have, I hope, a large circulation."

LONDON:
25, COLVILLE TERRACE, POWIS SQUARE, W.

FURNISH THROUGHOUT (Regd.)

OETZMANN & CO.,
67 TO 79 HAMPSTEAD ROAD
(Near Tottenham Court Road, London).
CARPETS, FURNITURE, BEDDING, DRAPERY, FURNISHING, IRONMONGERY, CHINA, GLASS, &c,
Orders per Post receive prompt and careful attention.

OETZMANN'S PATENT FOUR-HANDLED TOILET SERVICES.
Handles secure against breakage, convenient for lifting with both hands. Pours from any side. Readily handled from any position. Greater elegance of form. Pattern No. 103.

	s.	d.
In Cambridge Blue, on Ivory Wedgwood Ware, Single Set	10	6
In Plain Ivory, per Set	9	9
Other designs and colourings, from	11	9

STRONG BLACK & BRASS FRENCH BEDSTEAD & BEDDING, Complete.
With Double-woven Wire Spring Mattress, good Wool Mattress in Striped Tick, Bolster. and Leather Pillows, complete, 6 ft. 6 in. long.

WIDTH—3 ft., 45s. 6d.   3 ft. 6 in., 55s. 6d.   4 ft., 59s.   4 ft. 6 in., 63s.

Fitted Furniture, Artistic Paper Hangings, Painting, Decorating, Gas Fittings, Stoves, Ranges, &c., and every requisite for completely Furnishing a House throughout of any class.

ILLUSTRATED CATALOGUE.
THE BEST FURNISHING GUIDE EXTANT, POST FREE.

FURNISH THROUGHOUT (Regd.)

OETZMANN & CO.,

67 TO 79 HAMPSTEAD ROAD

(Near Tottenham Court Road, London).

CARPETS, FURNITURE, BEDDING, DRAPERY, FURNISHING, IRONMONGERY, CHINA, GLASS, &c.

Orders per Post receive prompt and careful attention.

OETZMANN'S PATENT DINNER SERVICES.

With self-supporting covers to the Dishes and Turens, entirely made china, metal fittings. Pattern No. 17, in Brown or Ivory Ware

50 Pieces	... ...	£1 5 0	70 Pieces	... ...	£23
101 Pieces	... ...	£3 3 3			

Price List of other Patterns on application.

THE "PRINCESS" WICKER CHAIR.

WALNUT ENVELOPE CARD TABLE.

Tastefully upholstered and draped in tapestry 11/
Settee to match 35/
A Large variety of Wicker Chairs, Settees, Lounges, Tables, &c.

Lined with cloth ... £2 17 6
Do., handsomely inlaid 3 7 6

Fitted Furniture, Artistic Paper Hangings, Painting, Decorating, Gas Fittings, Stoves, Ranges, &c., and every requisite for completely Furnishing a House throughout of any class.

ILLUSTRATED CATALOGUE.

THE BEST FURNISHING GUIDE EXTANT, POST FREE.

www.ingramcontent.com/pod-product-compliance
Ingram Content Group UK Ltd.
Pitfield, Milton Keynes, MK11 3LW, UK
UKHW042152280225
455719UK00001B/301